The Return of Merlin

Star Lore and the Patterns of History

Gordon Strachan

The Return of Merlin

Star Lore and the Patterns of History

Floris Books

First published in 2006 by Floris Books
© 2006 Gordon Strachan

British Library CIP Data available

ISBN-10 0-86315-553-7
ISBN-13 978-086315-553-6

Printed in Great Britain
By Biddles, King's Lynn

Contents

In memory of George Rankin

Acknowledgments

This book has had such a long gestation period it surprises me that it has finally come to birth. I am grateful to all those who, over the years, have contributed to the happy event of its final publication. Many years ago, the members of the Scottish Astrological Association, especially Mary Chalmers and Violet Milne, encouraged me to take my astrological studies further, and Dr Nicholas Grier, then Chairman, introduced me to the article by Charles Carter on which this book is based. Other astrologers have been helpful, especially Clare Martin, Melanie Reinhart, the Rev Pamela Crane, Caroline Gerard, Marie Louise Wiseman, Morelle Smith, Martin Davies and Roy Gillett, while Katherine Davies, Dawne Kovan, Dr Anthony Thorley and Peter Snow made valuable comments on the draft manuscript.

I shared my initial ideas about the connection between Charles Carter's theory of epochs and the historical Grail-Merlin literature with Dr Karen Ralls (née O'Keefe), then a post-graduate student, and carried this further in discussions with Ken Campbell and members of the Longtown (Cumbria) Arthurian Society. I am most grateful to them and to historian, Charles Lawrie, of Bangor, who helped put my knowledge of the Scottish Merlin stories on a firm footing.

In more recent years, I have found it very stimulating sharing various understandings and experiences of Merlin with Celtic bard, Fiona Davidson, Merlin scholar, Dr Gwen Enstem, Mark Oxbrow, Ean Begg, Stewart Keith, Welsh scholar, the Rev Gareth Davies, Richard Rudd and William and Heather Elmhirst.

I am also deeply indebted to my students in the Centre for Continuing Education at the University of Edinburgh. They have shared my Merlin and astrological enthusiasms, lent me books, researched details and debated topics. Among these I would like particularly to mention Isabel Lennie, Maurice Franceschi and the late George Rankin. I am also most grateful to Sarah Frost for drawing the maps, Andrew Gilmour for composing the astrological diagrams and Cumbrian artist, Meg Falconer, for permission to use her magical painting, *Merlin's Well,* on the front cover.

Elspeth, my wife, has been very supportive during the writing of this book and Christopher, my son, has encouraged my researches into

9

wizardology. There are other, mainly ecclesiastical, friends; I would have liked to thank them by name but they have preferred to remain anonymous.

I have dedicated the book to George Rankin, who died recently. He was a great friend, close colleague and Merlin enthusiast.

Preface

I have always believed that there are cycles in history. This got me into deep trouble during my first degree at Oxford. We were not encouraged to find patterns as our studies were supposed to be based on rigorous scientific analysis. When I served up an essay based on my understanding of Arnold Toynbee's *A Study of History,* in which he explains the reasons for the recurrent patterns that he observed in the rise and fall of civilizations, I was severely criticized. This was as much for attempting to find a pattern in history as for finding it in Toynbee, who as I was to find out later, was condemned by most historians. Others were also condemned for daring to *impose* a pattern on the empirical data. Gradually, I discovered the historical discipline, known as *historiography,* the study of the presuppositions of historians — but this too was forbidden territory. It wasn't taught at Oxford! I came to realize that it was banned because the degree course in which I was enrolled only held one important presupposition; that the development of history demonstrated the long and complex, but uniquely fascinating, rise of English imperial chauvinism, from Anglo-Saxon origins to world domination. Historiographical studies were frowned upon because they questioned this unexamined but universally accepted assumption. What I later realized was that this would all have been more acceptable to me if my degree had been called 'English History,' but it wasn't. It was called 'History.' It seemed petty to get upset by such a small difference in the title but was it any less petty or important than calling Britain England? Not to someone brought up in the London suburbs by Scottish parents and who, therefore, qualified for the title of London Scottish.

My tutor sensed that under my inarticulate questionings lurked a mind that was more concerned with philosophical, rather than historical questions, and that my historiographical, albeit Scottish nationalist, sympathies hid a theological bent. This leaning eventually became stronger and when I finally settled to a second degree in theology, it was at the University of Edinburgh. There, distracted by other enthusiasms and a general acceptance of the primacy of a theological, as distinct from a historical, worldview, I found that my questions regarding the cycles of history went onto the back burner. However, the topic rose up

again when my biblical studies hit the subject of what is usually called
Christian Apocalyptic. This is the theological topic concerning the End
of the World, the End Times, and is based on certain books of the Bible,
principally Daniel and Revelation. It has played a major role in Christian
consciousness from the first century to the present day. This consciousness was so pervasive among my evangelical and pentecostal Christian
friends that I came to realize that there is not much Christian understanding of history as such. There is only the history of the historic churches
and of the colossal volcano of anti-history, in the form of the seething
lava of apocalyptic, which has erupted from time to time into history,
usually with disastrous consequences.

For many years I accepted that this was the way it was and had to be.
Having tried to find a historical and a theological answer without success, I wouldn't have known where else to look. It never occurred to me
that the answer might be found in the stars. Astrology for me was a taboo
subject and rivalled tabloid pin-ups in cultural ostracism. It lost easily
because while the forbidden fascination with pin-up models was at least
understandable, astrology offered no such obvious attractions, being generally held to be full of unverifiable fabrications pedalled by charlatans to
the simple-minded and credulous. Nothing in my London-Scottish back-
ground, my historical or theological studies, had changed that.

Imagine my horror then when I discovered astrology in the Bible.
At the time I was studying the image of the New Jerusalem in the book
of Revelation and was deeply shocked when I realized that the twelve
jewels in the foundation of the Holy City as envisioned by St John,
were listed as the appropriate gemstones for the signs of the zodiac. At
the same time, because St John repeats this imagery from the books of
Daniel and Ezekiel, I realized that the zodiac permeated the Bible, and
even the so-called Four Living Creatures symbolized the four fixed signs
of the zodiac: Aquarius, Taurus, Leo and Scorpio. The fact that these
are also the symbols of the four Gospel writers — Matthew (Aquarius),
Mark (Leo), Luke (Taurus) and John (Scorpio) — sent me into deep
shock. Could St John the Divine have been a heretic? Or could it be that
I had uncovered a deep taboo against astrology in historical Christianity?
At the time I phoned a friend for counselling but he was equally upset.
He reacted like someone who had just been bereaved. He said 'Don't tell
anyone, will you?' I replied 'Certainly not!'

However, in time, we both changed our minds. I continued with
my study of the Bible and continued to suffer more shock-horror

when I discovered how much astrology there was in it, and when I realized to what lengths the translators of the New Testament from the original Greek into English had gone to pretend that it wasn't there. This was particularly the case in the consistent mistranslation of the words for *age* and *ages*. The Greek words are *aiōn* and *aiōnes*, from which we get our word aeons, meaning a long period of time. In the King James translation of the Bible, the Authorized Version of the early seventeenth century, both these words are translated 'world.' Yet, the Greek for world is *cosmos*, which is seldom used. This has been of enormous importance over the centuries because wherever the King James AV was read, which for centuries was the whole English-speaking world, sentences which should have been translated 'the end of the age' were instead mistranslated as 'the end of the world.' This consistent mistake, as in 'Lo, I am with you always, even unto the end of the world,' gave a huge apocalyptic spin to the New Testament expectation of the 'End Times.' It effectively robbed Christians of any historical perspective at all, and at the same time robbed the gospel of any meaningful astrological option. This is how it has been over the centuries and, among neo-conservatives in American politics, has had, and continues to have, quite literally an apocalyptic grip on the world.

I eventually had the courage to publish these, what I considered to be important, findings in 1987 under the title *Christ and the Cosmos,* and expected some negative response from Evangelicals and some affirmation from Liberal Christians, but I was mainly ignored. However, it sold sufficiently well to be revised and republished as *The Bible's Hidden Cosmology* in 2004. The most important difference in the new version being the inclusion of an essay by the famous astrologer, Charles Carter, which had been recommended to me by various astrologers who had enjoyed my original book but had found it too astrologically simple, not to say simplistic. Charles Carter's theory is simple but not simplistic. He divides the 2160 years of the Age of Pisces into twelve epochs of 180 years each, starting with Aries. These epochs explain the development of European history to a remarkable extent. I found this essay very important because it answered positively the question I had asked all those years ago, namely: were there cycles in history, and if so how can they be identified? In Carter I discovered that they can be traced to the movements of the stars. The fact that I did not so much find all this in astrology as that it was the result of astrology finding me from the Bible,

is deeply gratifying. I can claim with some certainty that Christian her-
esies, like academic fashions, go through cycles of rejection and acceptance and that what are often considered to be presuppositions written in
stone, turn out to have been written in the sand which the larger cycles
of time blow away, exposing a deeper level of understanding and a more
universal truth.

Introduction

Recent research into the ancient civilizations of Egypt and Babylon, and indeed of other cultures including that of Megalithic Britain, has shown that the movement of the stars was of supreme importance and, according to *Hamlet's Mill* by Giorgio de Santillana and Hertha von Dechend, and other related scholarly works, formed the basis of their mythology. What their gods and goddesses were doing was closely related to what the planets and constellations were doing. Their stellar observations were detailed and accurate. None more so than the extremely slow movement of the earth's spin against the sun and the stars, known as the *precession of the equinoxes*. This backward movement has been so forgotten by our modern educational system that many think that the longest movement of the earth is the year of 365 days. But this is not the case, for this backward movement of the earth, although very slow indeed, spins the earth like a top at the rate of 1° every seventy-two years. The completion of one whole cycle takes 25 920 years or thereabouts. This means that over long periods of time the fixed stars and constellations are not fixed, they move, as does the pole star. As Santillana and von Dechend show in *Hamlet's Mill* much of the world's mythology tells the story of how ancient people coped with their discovery that the earth wobbled on its axis and that the gods and goddesses of the celestial north changed every two thousand years. This book is not about this, because up to a point at least, I have dealt with that in *The Bible's Hidden Cosmology*. All that it is important to know is that this precession of the equinoxes forms a cycle of 25 920 years which is called the Great Year and that it was this that the ancient cultures divided into twelve Ages of 2 160 years each, according to the signs of the zodiac. These were known as the *aiōnes,* the aeons, which, because the whole cycle of precession went backwards, started with the aeon of Pisces, the fish, and ended with the aeon of Aries, the ram. Thus, the Age of Aries precedes the Age of Pisces. It is this cosmology which lies behind the New Testament affirmations, which state that Jesus was born either at the end of the Ages, *aiōnes* (not world), or at the end of the Age, *aiōn* (not world). The denial of this cosmology by two millennia of Christians, coupled with ruthless ecclesiastical inquisitions and witch hunts, is enough to justify the opinion of many ex-Christians today, as well as many of other faiths and none, who criticize the historical legacy of Christendom for having encouraged ignorance, prejudice and bigotry.

I found that the main section of society which accepted *Christ and the Cosmos* were the astrologers. It even paradoxically helped two of them at least to find their way back secretly to the Catholic Church! It was from astrologers that I received encouragement to carry on with my biblical-astrological studies. It was also astrologers who told me that the New Age was a concept that lacked astrological precision and that Charles Carter's essay, *Historical Cycles and Newly Found Planets*, could take me on to a more detailed exploration of the historical-astrological process.

In seven hundred years the laurel will be green again

The most attractive qualities of Charles Carter's essay were its brevity, its slender grasp of history and its justifiable modesty. However, what he had remembered did fit his theory of epochs sufficiently well for me to realize that he had hit on a theory, which was simple and yet which seemed to work. It was also one to which I could add significantly from my more recent studies of church, architectural and cultural history, which was gratifying. It must be remembered that Carter was first and foremost an astrologer and not a historian. It is, therefore, remarkable that his historical correlations are as relevant as they turn out to be, even if seemingly simplistic.

My realization that, for all its simplicity, Carter might have stumbled onto an important ancient system of astrological history dawned on me initially during a visit to Cathar country in the Languedoc. I had found the exploration of Montségur, the mountain, the castle and the village, most moving. Contemplating the monument to the horrendous massacre there in 1244, I was impressed by what seemed to be the modern fulfilment of a prophecy after seven hundred years. This prophecy, which I found featured on postcards, was very haunting. It read in the old language of Occitan: 'Mais, apretx sept cents ans verdejo lé laurier sur Cendrum des Martyrs!' (But in seven hundred years the laurel will be green again on the ashes of the martyrs!).

I was surprised to find that the popularity of the Cathars and of the pilgrimage to Montségur was of quite recent origin. Ean Begg in *The Search for the Holy Grail and the Precious Blood* put it well, saying that it:

stems largely from the combined interests of a school-
master of Tarascon, Antonin Gadal (1877–1962) and a
number of different esoteric groups which included German
Anthroposophists, Dutch Rosicrucians, the Polaires, the
White Eagle Lodge and Gadal's disciple, the enigmatic
Otto Rahn.

My old but latent interest in historical cycles was rekindled at
Montségur, especially by an eloquent comment of Ean Begg, which
matched my experience:

> The ruins of Montségur are as mysterious and beautiful
> today as ever, while the little town has reflowered (after
> seven centuries) into a new age Mecca like Glastonbury.

I found all that Ean Begg had observed very accurate. Even the
Catholic church was locked with only one mass a month advertised, while
the attractive little bookshops were full of material on the Cathars.

During my experience at Montségur, I made a mental note to measure up
the seven hundred years from 1244 and the Massacre to 1944, and the
famous visit of the enigmatic treasure hunter and SS Officer, Otto Rahn,
on Carter's zodiac of the epochs. However, in the meantime I received
what purported to be an ancient prophecy of Merlin from a Welsh-speak-
ing scholar, the Reverend Gareth Davies. This was to the effect that
Merlin and Arthur would return after seven hundred years:

> In 700 years, I will return with Arthur
> And the men of the north will arise
> They will find the North behind the north
> And Fortune will smile.[1]

Whether this could be verified academically was problematic. I was
unable to discover, but it was intriguing to say the least. What I did find
was, however, in itself exciting enough for when I counted out the years
between the time when the great stories about Arthur, Merlin and the
Round Table were written down in the late twelfth century and the time
when these events were supposed to have happened in history in the fifth
century, I found it to be approximately seven hundred years. Likewise,

when I counted out the years between the two Ages in Scottish history which have been called 'Great,' namely the Great Age of the Celtic Saints in the late sixth and early seventh century and the Great Age of the Wars of Independence, the late thirteenth and early fourteenth centuries, I found them to be approximately seven hundred years apart. On the strength of these and other developments from Charles Carter's theory of epochs, I decided to give the matter more time and research. The results are in the following pages.

The prominence of Arthur's Merlin in the English seven-hundred-year cycle and of the Caledonian Merlin in the Scottish cycle, are the main reasons why Merlin features in my title. The fact that there is another cycle being completed between the Great Age of the Scottish Wars of Independence and our present time, forms the basis, among other things, for my belief in Merlin's imminent return.

Visual aids for the astrologically challenged

Those who know a reasonable amount about astrology will find my text easy to understand. For those who do not, it may be a little harder. In order to help these I have included five explanatory charts for beginners. In these I have laid out the basic elements of astrology as clearly and simply as I can (Figs.1–5). For doing these and the other explanatory charts throughout the text, I am deeply grateful for the excellent computer graphics of Andrew Gilmour.

Prophetic disclaimer

I have very little to say about the predictions of Merlin, either as a result of his second-sight or his astrology. I am well aware that Geoffrey of Monmouth's first publication was *Prophecies of Merlin* in 1132 and that these were incorporated into his *History of the Kings of Britain* in 1136. Neither do I doubt that for many centuries Merlin's reputation rested mainly on the supposed veracity of his predictions concerning the political fortunes of the nation. I have read R.J. Stewart's commentary on these in his *Merlin: The Prophetic Vision.* Indeed I have studied them closely and found them very absorbing. Yet I have been left feeling that, while each of the prophecies may or may not be genuine and may or may not

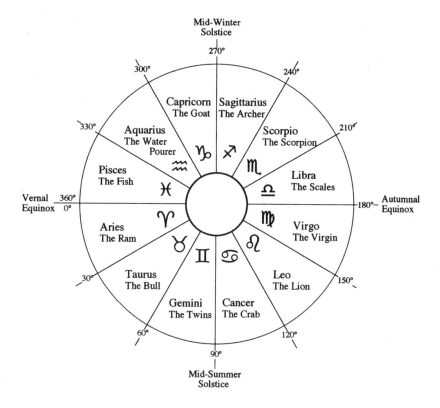

Fig.1 The signs of the zodiac

be accurately interpreted, it is of little consequence to me whether it is or it isn't. There is nothing specifically personal in this ambivalence for I have had exactly the same reaction to the prophecies of Nostradamus. Over the years I have accepted that what Nostradamus predicted about this or that, is of little consequence to me. Likewise with Merlin. This is not the fault of R.J. Stewart. On the contrary, I think he makes out a very good case for the veracity and importance of Merlin's prophecies. I certainly do not agree with George Buchanan's influential opinion of 1560 that he was 'an egregious imposter, and cunning pretender rather than a prophet' although for all Stewart's persuasiveness, I would agree with Buchanan to the extent that at least some of his vaticinations 'are obscure, and contain nothing certain, on which, before the event happens, any rational anticipation can be founded, or which, after it has happened, can be explained as a true prediction.'[2]

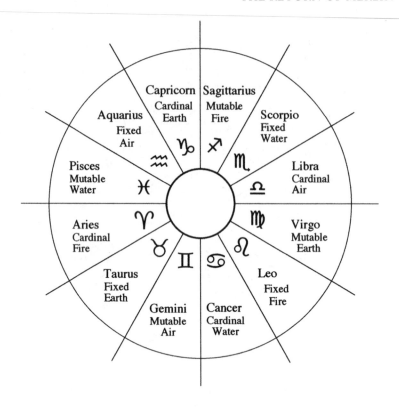

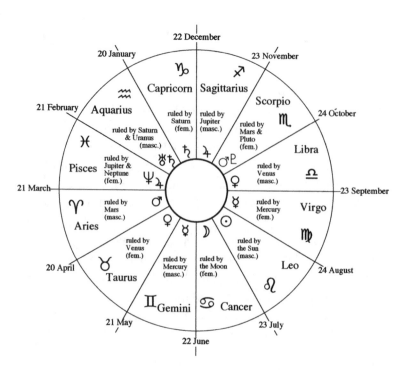

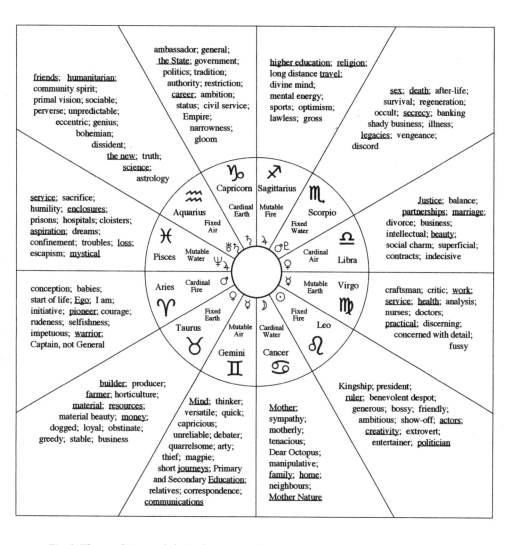

Fig.4 The qualities and their characteristics

*Fig.2 (opposite top) The triplicities (cardinal, fixed and mutable) and the
    quadruplicities (earth, air, fire and water)*

Fig.3 (opposite below) The planetary rulers

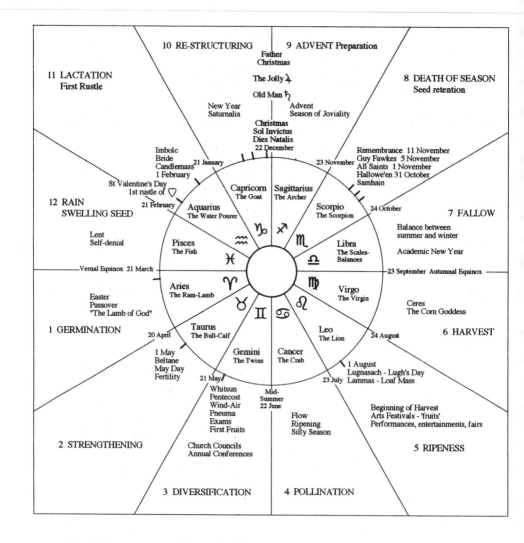

Fig.5 The seasons and festivals of the year

My inability to comment on the prophecies of Merlin comes not from my belief or disbelief. I am just unable to come to a conclusion at all. I am truly agnostic. I suppose I have to admit that the reputation of the Merlin who interests me does not depend on his gift of prediction. Merlin for me has never been an important predictive prophet. He has always been a mysterious figure who had magical gifts it is true but who represented a less clearly defined, but somehow more important, dimension of human personality. To my mind, he embodies a more highly developed intuition and imagination, a deeper perception, a deeper wisdom than most of us. Yet he is still part of us, he is not merely a conjurer doing his thing. I suppose I think of him as something like an archetype and that, also in the Jungian sense, his astrology is of an alchemical variety.

I have, therefore, sidestepped the issue of Merlin as a predictive astrologer and have attempted to rediscover him, to reinterpret him as a hermetic figure. I have tried to redefine him as a figure from the hermetic tradition, to be understood within the terms of that largely forgotten and largely discredited symbolism. I have been encouraged in this direction by realizing that largely forgotten and discredited though this tradition may be, it has come alive again in recent years for millions of younger people through the fantasy writings of J.K. Rowling. For who can doubt that much of her inspiration, such as the notion of the Philosopher's Stone, the Order of the Phoenix and the alchemist Nicolas Flamel, comes from this medieval, magical source.

1. Charles Carter's Theory of Piscean Epochs

Charles Carter's theory of Piscean epochs was first propounded, or perhaps 'proposed' is a more appropriate word, because he presented it so modestly, in an article, which first appeared in *Astrology* for December 1947. It was called 'Historical Cycles and Newly Found Planets.' To my knowledge, it was never expanded or developed in any way and still stands as an unappreciated essay in an otherwise greatly appreciated and highly acclaimed astrological career.

He begins his essay by admitting that it is very difficult to define periods of history. This is particularly so when it comes to attempting to demonstrate divisions of the Age of Pisces because there are so many opinions about when exactly it started, and also because there are, likewise, a great many options regarding its ending and the start-date for the Age of Aquarius. However, unlike other astrologers, who doubt whether there are *any* cycles in history other than those formed by the conjunctions of planets, he asserts that belief in them and in the succession of historical 'periods' ruled by the planets, was strong in Hindu astrology and that he agrees with this. He believes that there definitely *are* periods, or epochs, and that it is important to study them:

> However, it is certain that periods or epochs do occur and can be correlated with the signs. This will, I believe, be quite clear to those who have the astrological knowledge that will indicate to them what should be looked for. These periods are not only intensely interesting historically, but they also provide a background for all social and political studies, dominating as they do the entire life of their times.

What is most unexpected and indeed a risky procedure for such a distinguished astrologer, is that he then goes on to solve the knotty problem regarding the start-date of the Age of Pisces by making a bold claim. He does not go into details of the difficulties surrounding this, he just simply and boldly claims that *for him* it started with the year of the birth of Christ:

We begin, then, from AD 1 or thereabouts. The exact date of Jesus' birth is uncertain, but a matter of a few years is of small importance, for *Natura non agit per saltum* (Nature does not proceed by leaps) and we shall always find that one epoch tends to pass somewhat gradually into the next.

This is an enormous double claim, first to select what many astrologers would take to be an unjustifiably arbitrary date and then to choose the traditional Christian option. This would be dismissed as old fashioned and sentimental by those for whom the Star of Bethlehem story is considered to be no more than a pious fable. It is my belief that, although Carter himself makes no claim for it, the reason why his theory works so well is precisely because its start-date is the birth of Christ and that the division of the Age of Pisces into twelve epochs of 180 years each, also works well, because in some mysterious way, the twelve apostles of Jesus can be interpreted as twelve archons, or ancient lords of time under his Piscean leadership. I do not intend to develop this interpretation because I have already done something similar within a biblical framework in *The Bible's Hidden Cosmology*. It is sufficient to state that while some may feel I personally have wandered far from the Christian fold by taking astrology seriously, I would claim that the astrology I follow is derived from the Bible, and that it is much more central to biblical revelation than most Christians have been led to believe. It may be that my belief in Merlin and his return is much more problematic. That distinct possibility is at least relevant to this book, but will be considered later.

Charles Carter then goes on to divide the Age of Pisces into twelve epochs of 180 years. We will now examine a summary of this, the major part of his essay. I have added some of my own observations from church, architectural and cultural history which I found important, and which fitted well into Carter's system. In the text I have combined my additional material with Carter's but in the two illustrations I have separated them, to make it clearer what is mine and what was his.

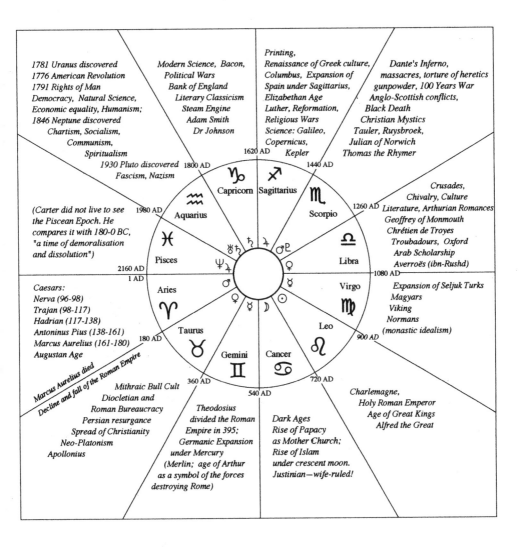

Fig.6 The Piscean epochs according to Charles Carter

Carter's historical evidence for the twelve Piscean epochs

In dividing the Age of Pisces into the twelve epochs of 180 years Carter says modestly that by so doing 'we may find ourselves able to carry out some useful researches into the correspondences that may be found between these epochs and the accepted values of the twelve zodiacal signs (or constellations).'

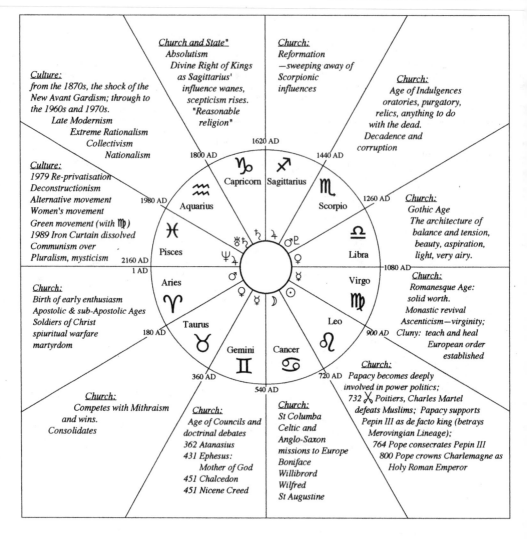

Fig.7 Church and cultural history based on Charles Carter's epochs

1. The first epoch AD 1–180 is that of the first sign Aries, the Ram, which is a cardinal fire sign ruled by Mars
It is the sign of the warrior, the initiator and the pioneer. Carter saw these qualities manifest supremely in the aggressive expansion of the Roman Empire under the despotism of the Caesars:

> This first epoch covers the period of the Caesars and their successors Nerva, Trajan, Hadrian and the two Antonines.

> It was a period during which absolute power lay in the hands of one man and that power was hardly disputed. ... It was an age of complete despotism except in so far as it was tempered by the fear of assassination or military revolt. This agrees well with Aries.

What Carter says about the Caesars is strangely mirrored in the birth and growth of the Christian Church. During the Aries epoch it had great energy and spread to all known countries. The Apostles and the Seventy-Two had the missionary drive of Aries pioneers. The Apostolic and post-Apostolic periods saw the soldiers of Christ fight many a spiritual battle while the cult of martyrdom, led by such figures as Polycarp and Justin, made heroes out of the fallen.

2. The second epoch, AD 180 to 360, is that of Taurus, the Bull

This is a fixed earth sign ruled by Venus and is associated with the builder, the farmer, material resources and physical beauty. Carter observes that it begins in 180 with the death of the philosopher-emperor Marcus Aurelius and that it was from this event that Gibbon dated the beginning of *The Decline and Fall of the Roman Empire*. The series of defeats at the hands of the barbarians, apart from the reign of Diocletian, signalled the end of the dominant influence of Aries, while the development of garrison legions building defences and 'digging in,' supported by an expanding bureaucracy, marked the increase of imperial stability in a very Taurean way. However, this eventually led to stagnation and decline.

On the religious side of things Carter notes the rise of the cult of Mithras, the Bull-slayer throughout the Roman Empire and also the strong influence of the Platonic and Pythagorean philosophical revival. These movements ran contemporaneously with the spread of Christianity and taken all together, showed that 'an ideal of saintliness had come into men's minds that would have seemed strange and unintelligible to the pagans of a century before.'

On the political scene at this time, Carter notes the important revival of the Persian Empire. This he believes is because Persia is ruled by Taurus:

> Now Persia is under Taurus, and it is very natural that in any given epoch, countries that come under the same sign-value as the epoch will in some respect experience an augmentation.

3. The third epoch, from 360 to 540, is that of Gemini, the Twins
It is a mutable air sign ruled by Mercury. Being an air sign and change-able, Gemini displays the mercurial qualities of quick wittedness, a magpie energy for collecting disparate knowledge and a passion for debate and/or argument. It rules primary and secondary education, com-munications and short journeys. Carter associates it with duality for the twins argue continuously and are often divided. This is exemplified by the Emperor Valentinian, who in 364 took the fateful step of dividing the Empire, giving the eastern part to his brother. The final division came after Justinian the Great (527–65).

Under the epoch of Gemini he also puts the rise of the Germanic races. This is of great importance to him and indeed to us:

> Perhaps the most striking thing about this period, from the general European point of view, was the dominance of the Germanic races. During the Taurus age they had per-petually harassed the Empire; now they flooded over it and left their traces in France, Spain, Northern Italy and even Africa. Tacitus says of the Germans that they worshipped Mercury before all other gods, and so this development seems in agreement with our hypothesis.

In Church history striking expressions of Gemini's capacity for argu-ment can be seen in the seemingly endless debates about exactly who Jesus was, how he should be described in credal formulae and who should be regarded as heretical! These debates were often fierce and acrimonious leaving lasting wounds and divisions in the Body of Christ. This was certainly the case with regard to Athanasius and the Athanasian Creed of 362; the Council of Ephesus regarding the doctrine of the motherhood of God in 431, the final adoption of the Nicene Creed and the definitive Christological formulae decided upon at the Council of Chalcedon in 451.

4. The fourth epoch is that of Cancer, the Crab, from 540 to 720
This is a cardinal water sign ruled by the moon. It is the sign of the mother and of all motherly qualities. It rules the family and the home as well as Mother Nature and Mother Church. Carter sees the rise of the Papacy under Pope Gregory the Great from 590 as very Cancerian and also the great influence which the Emperor Justinian's wife had on the Emperor:

One might expect some great female figures to occur during these times, but this was, of course, something that could not easily occur, taking into account the general level of civilization. However, one of the most famous monarchs of the time, Justinian, was notoriously wife-ruled. The same emperor has come down to us made famous by the legal codification that took place under his auspices and perhaps that has some connection with the exaltation of Jupiter in Cancer. It is the office of the law to protect the innocent and this protective aspect is quite Cancerian.

Carter also notes the rise of what he calls *Muhammedanism* but without comment. In this he reveals himself to be very much a man of his times, but may perhaps be forgiven for such a cursory mention because strictly speaking Islam would fall outside the scope of European history. However, this would not be tolerated today when Islam is increasingly recognized as having been an integral part of European development. For the purposes of this brief outline it is sufficient to mention that under the flag of the Cancerian crescent moon, Muslim armies had conquered Arabia, Egypt, Syria, Palestine, Iraq, Iran, Afghanistan, North Africa and Spain by the end of this epoch. They had become a force to be reckoned with throughout the world, including Europe.

5. The fifth epoch is that of Leo, the Lion, from 720 to 900
This is a fixed fire sign ruled by the sun. It is associated with kingship and fatherhood. It rules creativity, entertaining, acting and politicians. Carter sees it quite simply as the Age of Kings:

We are still in the Dark Ages, but the coronation of Charlemagne by the Pope, as Holy Roman Emperor, in the year 800 is an event of the first importance and thoroughly in accord with the Leo epoch. Indeed an age of great kings and emperors confronts us, just as, in the time of Aries' predominance, there were the figures of the Caesars. Under the guidance of these rulers the nations of Europe, arising from the broken remnants of the old empire, take shape. Above all, the French nation begins its

career appropriately under a Leo note. In England, at this
time, we have Alfred the Great.

It is of current political interest that some astrologers regard the tim-
ing of the coronation of Charlemagne as the first horoscope of a United
Europe. This is seen as the birth of Europe.

6. The sixth epoch is Virgo, the Virgin, from 900 to 1080

It is a mutable earth sign ruled by Mercury. Virgo is the craftsman, the
critic and the healer. She is practical and particular, and rules doctors,
nurses and all servers. Carter is strangely silent, finding little to say about
this epoch, declaring its Virgoan traits to be 'only obscurely characterized.' He lists the Magyar conquest of Hungary, the Viking invasions and
the Norman conquest of England in 1066 but without much conviction.
Then, rather half-heartedly, he mentions the Seljuk Turks:

> But perhaps one may note the coming into prominence of
> the Seljuk Turks. Turkey is said to be ruled by Virgo and
> this may be a racial, not a territorial, rulership.

Now here, not for the first time, I find myself so stimulated by the
striking correspondences which Carter does make, that I am frustrated
and perplexed by those that he does not make. Again, we must acknowledge that astrology was his area of expertise rather than history, which
would explain why he doesn't see the correspondence between the
Virgoan ruler Mercury and the revival of the monastic ideal during the
Virgoan epoch, as there is a strong link between Mercury-Hermes and
the archetype of the hermit. Monks and monasteries embody and insti-
tutionalize these hermetic qualities on a grand scale, and produced the
most important spiritual and cultural movement of the epoch. The same
Hermetic-Mercurial forces, which swept the north European tribes to
victory over the Roman Empire in the fifth century, returned in the tenth
to lay the firm foundations of the Europe we know today as a definable
Christian cultural entity.

Centred at Cluny in northern France from 910 and growing for the
two centuries of the Virgoan epoch, there was a massive resurgence of
monasticism spreading throughout Europe. Teaching, healing, ordering and highly disciplined, it was the embodiment of Virgoan Christian

spirituality as were its principles of strict ascetic virginity and obedi-ence. The rise of Romanesque architecture likewise with its fortress-like weight, solid foundations, round arches and static forms, epitomized the well-ordered virtues of this earthy practical sign. As its name implies, the Romanesque Age looked back to the Roman period and built to endure.

In addition, given his astrological standpoint, Carter's tentative refer-ence to the westward expansion of the Seljuk Turks in the latter half of this period is remarkably perceptive. He is much righter than he knew, as the historic and fateful results of that expansion closed the pilgrim routes for Christians going to the Holy Land and also threatened Constantinople. It was these developments, which in turn triggered off the First Crusade and led on to some of the main features of the next epoch of Libra.

7. The seventh epoch is Libra, the Scales, from 1080 to 1260

This is a cardinal air sign, ruled by Venus and is associated with the scales of justice, the balance of opposites, culture and beauty. It rules all partnerships; marriages, romantic liaisons, business and social rela-tionships. In contrast to the Virgoan epoch, Carter finds Libran qualities clearly manifest in the Libran epoch:

> The Libra epoch begins about 1080 and is, in my view, very clearly shown indeed. Literature and culture revive, and we come to the age of chivalry and romance. In 1096 we have the First Crusade. Doubtless most of the Crusaders were ruffians, at least by our standards, but it is still true that their expeditions were, at any rate for the best of them, inspired by an ideal.
>
> In 1110 my conspectus mentions one of the first of the miracle plays as being performed, and in 1139 Geoffrey of Monmouth's *History of the Britons,* the basis of all the vast literature of the Arthurian romances, is in existence.
>
> The University of Salerno is said to have been founded in 1150 and the same date is given approximately for the appearance of the Teutonic epic, the *Nibelungenlied.* In 1160 Chrétien de Troyes, one of the great French poets of the period of romance, flourished. The University of Paris was founded about 1210.

One must not overlook Arabian scholarship. Then there
were the troubadours and minnesingers, Walther von der
Vogelweide flourished around the beginning of the thirteenth century. William of Lorris wrote the *Romaunt of the
Rose* about 1237 which brings us to the close of the period.
Fortunately the cultural seeds sown in the Libra time continue to produce their flowers into this day.

Although Carter does not give any examples of Libran seeds which
are still producing their flowers, we could speculate that he might have
been referring for instance to Wagner's *Ring Cycle* as a late flowering
of the *Nibelungenlied*, to the passion of Victorian artists for romantic
depictions of Grail knights and, among other more recent retellings of
the story of Arthur, to T.H. White's *The Once and Future King*.

From what we have already noted about the epoch of Libra, all that
Carter refers to as exemplifying Libran characteristics rings true.
Indeed, it was such a seminal time that it is possible to add many more
examples which he fails to mention. The most arresting of these is the
rise of the Gothic cathedrals. There is an extraordinary synchronicity
between the main publications of the Arthurian-Grail literature and the
equivalent pioneering work in Gothic architecture. For instance during
the time when Geoffrey of Monmouth was writing *The Prophecies of
Merlin* and his *History* — that is, 1130–36 — Sens, the first complete
Gothic cathedral, was being built. During the time he was research-
ing *The Life of Merlin,* Abbot Suger was doing his influential Gothic
restorations at St Denis in Paris (1140s), and during the time of the
publications of the romances of Chrétien de Troyes, Robert de Boron
and Wolfram von Eschenbach 1170–1225, Chartres cathedral was
being built along with many other Gothic foundations such as Paris,
Senlis and Laon.

This remarkable synchronicity seems entirely appropriate because
the Arthurian-Grail literature and the Gothic cathedrals both express
Libran qualities in different ways. For instance the former, as historical
romances, express the Libran association with partnerships, with marriage and romance. Libra is a masculine sign but is ruled by Venus the
goddess of love. This is why it rules the creative balance or marriage of
opposites. Likewise the Gothic cathedrals exemplify the same balance
of opposites in the dynamic tension between the two arcs of the Gothic

arch, and the flying buttresses and pinnacles, without which the soaring structures would have fallen apart. The stained glass and rose windows exemplify the Libran quality of beauty, while the increasing height of the buildings bear witness to the physical expression of the spiritual aspiration of its cardinal air energies, reaching up to heaven. The fact that in the Period of Transition between Romanesque and Gothic almost all the new cathedrals were built after fires on their original Romanesque foundations, shows that the Gothic would not have been possible without the solid enduring strength and disciplined craftsmanship of the preceding epoch of Virgo.

8. The eighth epoch is that of Scorpio, the Scorpion, from 1260 to 1440
This is a fixed water sign ruled by Mars and its new ruler is Pluto, the god of the Underworld. It is associated with death and the after-life, with survival and regeneration. It rules sex, banking, legacies, illness, vengeance, secrecy, discord, torture and the occult. Carter finds many of these qualities to be prominent during this epoch:

> Assuming that Scorpio takes over about 1260, we have the massacre of the Sicilian Vespers in 1282, and before that, in 1252, Innocent IV approved the use of torture for the discovery of heresy. This period also covers the first use of gunpowder, a compound that was the first of so many deadly agencies.
>
> The Hundred Years War between France and England began in 1338 and ended a few years after the epoch of Scorpio. We have also endless Anglo-Scottish conflicts. Very characteristic was the Black Death which reached England in 1349 and had immense social consequences.
>
> A higher aspect of the sign is seen in the development in this age of Christian mysticism; one finds such names as Tauler, Ruysbroek, Julian of Norwich.

Once again, it is disappointing but understandable that Carter makes no mention of church developments except for the mystics. For instance, this was the epoch which saw the rise of the Sale of Indulgences granting time off Purgatory, the building of oratories and chantries where prayers were said for the dead, the traffic in relics and the increasing corruption which surrounded these Scorpio characteristics.

9. The ninth epoch is that of Sagittarius, the Archer, from 1440 to 1620
This is a mutable fire sign ruled by Jupiter. It is associated with higher
education, religion and long distance travel. Its characteristics are mental energy, optimism and over-indulgence. This epoch covers the Italian
Renaissance, the Reformation and the world-wide expansion of Europe,
so Carter finds it easy to identify these Sagittarian developments:

> The first item on my conspectus is 1440 itself, and under
> it the entry: Invention of Printing with movable types by
> Coster at Haarlem. It was not until 1475 that the first book
> was printed in the English language.
>
> In 1453 Constantinople fell to the Turks and as a conse-
> quence Greek refugees spread the ancient culture of their
> race over the west.
>
> The Western Hemisphere was opened up by Columbus in
> 1492 and a long list of dates of eminent geographical dis-
> coveries and feats of exploration could easily be compiled,
> were this necessary. However, these achievements are com-
> mon knowledge: what must be stressed is that the dominant
> power, and the one most active in opening up and subduing
> the New World, is that of Spain — a Sagittarian country.
>
> Moreover, much of the period is known to us as the
> Elizabethan Age, and it is probable that that monarch was
> the outstanding figure of the whole age. Her correct ascend-
> ant is Capricorn, but she had Jupiter in Sagittarius.
>
> It would be natural to expect religion to play a great
> part in a Sagittarian epoch; and so indeed it does. Martin
> Luther published his theses at Wittenberg in 1517 and the
> Reformation rapidly gathered strength. This again is com-
> mon knowledge and there is no need to dwell upon the
> subject, which nevertheless is as characteristic of the ninth
> sign as is the spirit of exploration and adventure.

Carter goes on to identify the Sagittarian signature in the cult of the
beard and of the padded doublets at the end of this epoch. These exag-
gerated the parts of the body ruled by Sagittarius! He also notes that
Jupiter the ruler of this epoch was probably behind the Peasants' Revolt
in Germany in 1524 and the founding of the Jesuits in 1539. He also
claims that the early experiments in natural science were Jupiterian:

There are also the beginnings of natural science in the modern sense. In 1589 Galileo was dropping cannon balls from the leaning tower of Pisa to disprove the Aristotelian doctrine that the speed of falling bodies is determined by their weight. Soon after he was using the telescope — a typically Jovian instrument — and the wonders of the heavens were being revealed in a manner hitherto undreamed of. Copernicus' *De Revolutionibus* had been printed some forty-six years earlier. Kepler began publishing in 1609, towards the end of this epoch.

10. The tenth epoch is that of Capricorn, the Goat, from 1620 to 1800

This is a cardinal earth sign ruled by Saturn. It is the sign of the statesman, the ambassador and the scientist. Its characteristics are authority, ambition and status. It rules empire, the civil service and rank. Carter sees it plainly stamped on this epoch in the rise of the European Empires, based on the explorations of the world under the previous epoch. He believes the literary and architectural classicism of the period, has a strong Saturnian connection as do the Puritan revolutions of the seventeenth century. He puts these and the Thirty Years war in Germany down to the influence of Mars, which is exalted in Capricorn. Likewise the firm establishment of modern science, beginning with Bacon's *Novum Organum* in 1620, is attributable to painstaking Capricornian analysis. He finds the founding of the Bank of England in 1694 a very Saturnian event, as is the industrial development of the iron industry and inventions such as the steam engine.

11. The eleventh epoch is that of Aquarius, the Water Carrier or Water Pourer, from 1800 to 1980

This is a fixed air sign whose old ruler like Capricorn is Saturn but whose new ruler is Uranus which was only discovered in 1781. Following the astrological belief that after a new planet is discovered its influence is widely felt and its attributes can be discerned in contemporary events, Carter believes that the epoch of Aquarius was hastened by the discovery of Uranus, who was quickly assigned to be its new ruler. Thus, apart from its old ruler Saturn and the characteristics associated with the tenth house as listed above, Aquarius is believed to carry the new attributes of Uranus, namely unpredictable revolution, eccentricity and bohemian genius. In a word it is associated with 'the new' and of course is the planet of the coming new Age of Aquarius. The eleventh sign is the sign of friendship, humanitarian and community spirit, of liberty, equality and fraternity, of science and astrology — for the ruler of astrology is Urania. Carter finds the attributes of Aquarius written large over this epoch:

> But the advent of Aquarius is hastened, or at least complicated, by the discovery of Uranus in the year 1781. Already in 1776 there had been the American Declaration of Independence and this was virtually carried into effect by 1781, when Lord Cornwallis surrendered to a Franco-American army at Georgetown.
>
> But the Capricorn 'influence' lasted well. That very Saturnian work, *The Decline and Fall of the Roman Empire,* was first published in 1776, and so also was Adam Smith's *Wealth of Nations.* James Watt patented his steam engine in 1782, and as the epoch ended we come to a veritable revolution, or spate of revolutions, in literature, economic life and politics. Once again there is no need to particularize but, as regards literature, it may be observed that Johnson died and Burns' first volume of poems was printed in the same year, 1786.
>
> Louis XVI was executed in 1793. Thomas Paine's *Rights of Man,* a most Aquarian work, had appeared two years earlier.
>
> So we come to the beginning of an Aquarian epoch in 1800. Not the Aquarian Age ... Of this Aquarian epoch which began in 1800 or thereabouts and will persist until 1980, we know enough without there being any need whatever to examine its trends in detail ... An incredible development of natural science has occurred and there has been a movement towards economic equality and the ideals of humanism, horribly interrupted, it is true, in our own day. This interruption we would like to ascribe to the entry into the human consciousness of the planet Pluto, the bringer to light of that which lies hidden. When humanity has adjusted itself to that fresh value, the present collapse of international morality may pass away and give place to something more ideal than Europe has previously known.

This last point refers to the effect of the discovery of Pluto in 1930 and its manifestation in the contemporary rise of fascism through Europe, as embodied in the dictators Franco, Mussolini and above all Hitler.

Carter died before the epoch of Aquarius ended in 1980 and so can hardly be accused of not doing justice to the eleventh house, particularly in a short essay which was probably originally given as only one lecture. He did not mention the concept of the 'Avant Garde' in the arts and in culture generally, which from the 1870s onwards became the major theme right through to the excesses of the 1970s, and is still very much with us today. The 'shock of the New' leading to novelty and eccentricity for its own sake, is surely very much an excessive expression of Aquarius' new ruler Uranus.

12. The twelfth epoch is that of Pisces, the Fishes, from 1980 to 2160

This is a mutable water sign, whose old ruler is Jupiter and whose new ruler is Neptune. It is the sign of the dreamer, the mystic and the suffering servant. Its characteristics are humility, sacrificial service and loss. It is associated with enclosures, cloisters, hospitals, prisons and all those who work in them. Carter did not live to see the transition from the Aquarian to the Piscean epoch, so I will attempt to do so for him. In the spirit in which he identified major synchronicities between the sign and the epoch, I will do likewise.

The first thing I notice is that the term 'Post Modernism' began to be used, eclipsing the earlier notion of 'Late Modernism,' around 1980; in other words, on cue. Post Modernism, under the influence of Neptune, the new ruler of Pisces, started to dissolve the rigid mechanistic structures set up by Saturn during the previous 360 years. This has been especially noticeable in the overthrow of the collectivist tyranny of Communism and the dogmatism of socialism which has been replaced by the more flexible concept of the mixed economy. This trend has been equally noticeable in the growth of relativism and pluralism in philosophical and religious fields.

Pisces is a feminine sign and as such I would ascribe the Women's Movement to her and to her opposite yet complementary sign Virgo. Together, I believe, they have also been responsible for the Green Movement and for the growth of general awareness that the earth's resources should no longer be regarded merely as commodities but as integral parts of a living holistic ecosystem personified by the earth goddess, Gaia.

Pisces is the mystic and the dreamer as mentioned, and it is truly remarkable that, if we look back to the Piscean epoch of the last Cosmic Age, that is, to the 180 years before the birth of Jesus Christ, we find the emergence of similar mystical characteristics. After two centuries of scepticism and rationalism, very like those which we have recently passed through, which we have associated with the epochs of Capricorn and Aquarius, there was a revival of very Piscean attributes in the resurgence of the ancient Mystery religions, especially in their belief in revelation through dreams. Martin Hengel, in *Judaism and Hellenism*, describes the spirit of those times, of which the Essenes were a notable example:

> The revival of piety after the collapse of traditional forms of religion in the *polis* and the wave of destructive scepticism in the fourth and third centuries BC, have as a typical feature the personal tie of the individual to particular deities, a tie which was grounded more strongly than in the earlier period through personal supernatural experiences, dreams, epiphanies, healings, direct instructions from God, etc.

This could be a description of what is happening today! The long wave of destructive scepticism since eighteenth-century rationalism, has undermined the traditional churches whose membership has declined drastically. On the other hand the growth of interest in alternative spiritual paths and what might loosely be called New Age consciousness, in which experience of dreams has been central since the time of Freud and especially Jung, has been very great. Epiphanies, associated with the experiences of spiritual gifts in Pentecostal and charismatic churches, and in the counter-culture with shamanism, have also been considerable. Likewise the development of healing 'miracles' through complementary medicines and the awareness of divine entities through channelling and out-of-body experiences, have all contributed to an enormous rise in mystical consciousness, which is very new and very Neptunian.

From all these developments, I would list the three main characteristics which have emerged during the first twenty-five years of the Piscean epoch as, first, pluralism; second, mystical experiences and third, its negative counterfeit — the destructive experiences caused by drug abuse. This third characteristic is so well known that, as Carter would say, it does not need to be detailed, yet perhaps it is important to stress that if the mystical and esoteric aspects of the monotheistic religions, had not been either marginalized, condemned as heresy or laughed at by mainstream orthodoxy in religion and science over so many centuries, it might have been possible to introduce our younger generations to the real experience of mystical spirituality which they lack instead of allowing the counterfeit to destroy them. This may be where astrology could help. This may be where the study of the stars and of ancient star lore could bring hope. This may be where the identification of cosmic patterns amidst the apparent random flux of life could bring a sense of purpose.

Can we recognize a pattern in the outline of European history as Charles Carter has defined it? Is it convincing or is it merely his own subjective selection of facts, which he has imposed on a meaningless plethora of historical data? The only way this question can be answered is if his selection of facts is convincing. Is his essay on the twelve epochs of the Piscean Age worthy of serious examination and possible approval?

For myself, I am convinced not only by the immense amount of major historical events and movements which seem to fit Carter's pattern but also by the great number of equally important events which he has left out, but which I have been able to add! He has shown that despite the profound scepticism with which patterns of history and astrology are generally regarded, it is possible to discern a pattern which might well bear closer scrutiny and help us to feel part of the continuously unfolding purposes of God from the past to the future.

Indeed I confess that I have found this to be so much the case that I have added my own material until it has become a book. It may be predictable that the book would turn out to be about Merlin because normal historians would be entitled to consider Carter's theory both simplistic and barmy, while normal people often take the Merlin stories as no more than medieval fables. They might judge that to find meaning in either could be a particular form of madness, while to compound them is the expression of an extreme form of lunacy. But they would be Muggles, wouldn't they, and this book is definitely *not* for Muggles.

Fig.8 Merlin, the enchanter (Louis Rhead, 1923)

2. Merlin and Arthur in Star Lore

Prominent in Charles Carter's list of important Libran manifestations between 1080 and 1260 is the publication of Geoffrey of Monmouth's *History of the Britons* in 1139. Its full title was *The History of the Kings of Britain,* and although scholars disagree as to its exact date of publication, some giving it as 1136[3] and others 1135[4], all agree that it did indeed form the 'basis of all the vast literature of the Arthurian romances.'[5] It would not be too much to say that it was this book which marked the literary 'birth' of Arthur because, although there had been a long gestation period going back to the ninth-century chronicler, Nennius, it was only through Geoffrey of Monmouth's *History* that Arthur began life as a national, and then an international, hero.

This was even more the case for Merlin because, until that time, he had had no definite independent existence. Like Arthur, he had also featured prominently in Nennius' *History of the Britons,* but he had not been called Merlin. He had been confused with the British leader Ambrosius Aurelianus who was also thought to have possessed prophetic powers. Nennius makes out that, in the story of the discovery of the dragons fighting under King Vortigern's tower, the king was frightened of Ambrosius' youthful display of magic powers, because he also had political power. Ambrosius is known in Welsh as *Emrys Gwledig* and Nennius gives him that title. *Gwledig* is Welsh for a regional ruler and can also mean prince.[6]

Geoffrey of Monmouth retells Nennius' old Welsh story but with a significant difference. His young seer is not the same as the historical commander Ambrosius or Emrys. Instead he calls him Merlin and creates another character who *is* the rightful prince Aurelius Ambrosius, the king of the Britons after Vortigern. For a while he says that Merlin 'was also called Ambrosius' but then he drops the double characterization. From then on his Merlin has his own identity as the wonder-worker who prophecies a Celtic resurgence, sets up Stonehenge and causes the birth of Arthur.[7]

From this unpromising historical confusion, Merlin makes his debut as an independent character, along with Arthur making the most impressive and long-running double act on the stage of British mythology.

Fig.9 Vortigern's castle at Dinas Emrys, North Wales

Indeed, his historical roots are so shaky that we may wonder how it was that such a confusing start should lead to the evolution of such an enduring, powerful and popular British legend.

My understanding of his extraordinary development lies in my belief that Merlin represents the embodiment of the archetype of the magician and that as such he is linked to the mythology associated with the planet Mercury. My reasoning for this is, in the first instance, that although he only arose as an independent character out of a confusion with the *gwledig* Ambrosius, this confusion nevertheless gives us a link with Mercury. Mercury's Greek name was Hermes and the Welsh for Hermes is Emrys and the Latin for Emrys is Ambrosius. Thus the identity between Merlin-Emrys or Ambrosius and Hermes-Mercury, though lost in translation, is plain. We will never know whether their original confusion of identity was genuine. Nevertheless, the more we learn about the character of the independent Merlin, as it develops throughout the growing *corpus* of Arthurian literature after 1136, the more he can be recognized as the embodiment of the Mercurial attributes of wisdom, prophecy, shape-shifting, trickster, riddler and sudden disappearer.

If this identification of Merlin Ambrosius with Emrys-Hermes can be accepted, then it explains most of the episodes in Geoffrey of Monmouth's stories about him, particularly with regard to the building of Stonehenge, which Geoffrey attributes to his magic, for as John Michell explains, there was an old legend which claimed that Stonehenge had been built by none other than Ambrosius:

> The Greek Hermes may be compared with the British Emrys, whose name is preserved at Stonehenge in that of its legendary builder, Ambrosius, and that of the neighbouring town Amesbury. Hermes is Ἑρμης, and Emrys transcribed in Greek letters is Ἐμρης, so the two words have the same letters and consequently the same value 353.[8]

Fig.10 Merlin creating Stonehenge, in an illustration for a fourteenth-century romance in the British Museum

Fig.11 Stonehenge

John Michell goes on to show that if 353 is taken as a unit of either 3.52 feet or 3.52 yards, then multiples of these units can be identified throughout the design of Stonehenge. The number symbolism known as 'Gematria,' allows for a convention called 'colel' whereby one unit may be added or subtracted from the value of the number without affecting its symbolic meaning. This is very much the case with the Sarsen stone circle:

> The average length of each lintel stone is 10.57 feet or 3.52 yards; the measured width, $3^1/_2$ feet, is doubtless intended to be 3.52 feet, a third of the length. The average interval between the upright pillars is 3.52 feet and the pillars them-selves are each 7.04 feet (3.52×2) wide.[9]

The attribution of the building of Stonehenge to Ambrosius-Hermes is thus suggested by the incorporation of multiples of the number of his name 353, into the ancient design. This in all probability accounts for the remark-able assertion in *The White Book of Rhydderch* that the very first name by which Britain was known was 'Myrddin's Precinct.'[10] It could also relate to Caesar's observation that Hermes-Mercury was considered to be the chief deity of the Gauls: 'The God they reverence most is Mercury.'[11]

In traditional star lore, this would mean that, astrologically speaking, Britain's ruler was Mercury-Hermes. This would then explain how, mythologically, Merlin developed a life of his own and continues to do so. In this respect he may be considered as an archetype in the Jungian sense. On this presupposition we may therefore go on to ask what were the mythological-astrological circumstances, as distinct from the historical ones mentioned above, which occasioned his 'birth' in 1136 or thereabouts. I believe that the answer to this lies in the resurgence of the ancient mythology of Mercury-Hermes, which was

Fig.12 Mercury-Hermes woodcut showing his caduceus

seeping into north-western Europe from the world of Islam in the early twelfth century. It formed part of what was known as the revival of the hermetic tradition, named after the figure of Hermes-Mercury himself, which incorporated the astral mythology of many cultures especially that associated with the Egyptian god Thoth.

I believe it was the pervasive percolation of this profoundly syncretistic tradition from Islamic lands, especially Spain, Sicily and Palestine which reactivated the old British legends, and which caused them to come alive again with a renewed vigour. I believe that the 'very ancient book written in the British language,' which Geoffrey claimed had been given to him by a certain Archdeacon Walter of Oxford, and which he also claimed had been his source for his *History,* may well have been a hoax since neither the said cleric nor his book have ever been identified.[12] It may also have been a decoy, putting scholars off the scent of a real but secret knowledge which was filtering into Geoffrey's consciousness, and out of which the important added extra dimensions of his stories came. This 'book' was perhaps the *Corpus Hermeticum* which was largely unknown and had to be because it was heterodox, being astrological and from the Sufis of Islam who were officially the infidel 'enemy' in those Crusading times. This may be the untold story behind Geoffrey's secret source and the secret agent from whom it came can in all probability be identified as the famous Arabic scholar and traveller, Adelard of Bath.

Adelard of Bath and the emerald ring

Although there is no record that Geoffrey of Monmouth ever met Adelard of Bath, they had much in common. They were almost exact contemporaries and died within a couple of years of each other in 1152 and 1150 respectively. They also shared the same patron in Robert, Earl of Gloucester, son of Henry I and half-brother of the Empress Matilda. This Robert supported Matilda staunchly in the civil war with Stephen, until his death in 1147. They were also both scholars on the cutting edge of new scholarship.

Compared with Geoffrey, Adelard was the more famous, being celebrated as a traveller and scholar, particularly of Arab lands, as well as a translator of classical Arab and Greek texts from Arabic to Latin. He is known to have travelled to Greece, Palestine, Southern Italy, Sicily and

Spain, and it is significant that most of these — particularly, the Holy Land. Sicily and Spain — are known to have been the three main sources from which syncretistic Hermeticism was filtering through from Islamic centres into Western Christian Europe at that time.

In 1130 he was known to have been back in England and by that time had already translated two astronomical and three astrological works. Sometime after 1126 he translated the astrological tables of al Khwaraizmi, the famous astronomer from Central Asia who worked in Baghdad in the ninth century. For the first time these tables made it possible for accurate horoscopes to be cast, which was important, among other things, to enable doctors to know when it was auspicious to let blood or attempt surgery.

The work for which Adelard became, and still remains most famous, is his translation of the geometrical *Elements* of Euclid. Yet, as Margaret Gibson points out, this attribution is not strictly accurate for it had already been done in Sicily. Adelard's fame lay not in the translation itself but in the *Exposition* of Euclid, which became widely influential.[13] It was at this time, the 1130s, that the first experiments in what was later called 'the Gothic style' took place, and it has been argued that it would have been impossible to teach aspiring masons how to build pointed arches and cross-ribbed vaults without first having taught them the more sophisticated use of compasses, which had not been needed for Romanesque style buildings. Adelard's pioneering importance with regard to geometry was thus twofold; firstly, it made the building of the Gothic style possible and secondly, it encouraged the development of accurate horoscopes. The ten horoscopes that are known to have been done for Henry I and members of his court have been attributed to him.

Adelard's place in the history books is thus secure, yet there is no evidence that he ever met Geoffrey of Monmouth. Therefore how can it be maintained that his Arab scholarship was so influential for Geoffrey? The thesis must remain speculation, it cannot be proved. Nevertheless there is one clue to this, which is very profound symbolically.

In Adelard's book on natural philosophy and theology, the *Quaestiones Naturales,* he portrays himself wearing a green cloak and also an emerald ring, a *smaragdus,* which he said was 'less extensive but more efficacious.' By the end of the twelfth century such gems, carved with astrological or amuletic signs, were common and were indications of the widespread acceptance of the Hermetic influence of those times. However, as Margaret Gibson tells us, in the 1120s and

1130s they were rare. What is even rarer and of great importance to a deeper understanding of Adelard is that the green cloak and the *smaragdus* ring symbolized Islam, in general, and the Sufis, in particular. For green is the sacred colour of the former and the emerald, *smaragdus* stone is the most important symbol of the latter. This was because in the tradition of Sufi mysticism, which was enjoying a revival at that time, a green mystical light had been seen during the many out-of-body journeys recorded at that time. It had been seen as part of transforming experiences claimed throughout the twelfth century through the nine spheres of the heavens, shining like a sort of inner aurora borealis, in the midst of a profound cosmic darkness. The Sufis who experienced this came from the revival of neo-Zoroastrian Platonism associated with the school of the Iranian Sufi-masters, Sohravardi and Najm Kobra, and, as Henry Corbin explains in *The Man of Light in Iranian Sufism,* was called 'the *visio smaragdina,* a specific degree of visionary apperception of outbursts of green light.'[14]

The location in which these experiences were believed to have taken place was between the eighth and ninth spheres in the confines of the celestial north pole, in the ambiance of the constellations of the Great and Little Bear. These were the circumpolar constellations near the celestial pole, whose pointer stars led directly to the pole itself, the hub and axis of the universe of the stars.

Thus Adelard's emerald ring, though seeming a small clue, may reveal that he was privy to the most profound secrets of the contemporary Sufis of Islam and that, to those who knew, he was not afraid to show it. Furthermore, it can be seen as leading to the heart of the myth which Geoffrey was telling in story-form when he tells us about the birth of Arthur by means of Merlin's magic. For the *smaragdus,* the emerald stone, is sacred to the goddess Artemis. Artemis is the goddess of the Great Bear. She is the Great She Bear of Greek mythology and her son is Arcas, the star Arcturus. He is the Son of the Bear and his name in ancient British star lore is Arthur. Arthur means Bear. He is our 'King Arthur.'

So the *smaragdus,* the emerald gemstone ring, tells us that Adelard was not just a great Arabic translator-scholar but that he knew star lore, the astral mythology which it symbolized. It also meant that, in all probability, he knew about the Emerald Tablet of the Hermetic Corpus. This was the name given to the central axiom 'As above, so below' or as in the little world, the microcosm, so in the great world, the macrocosm.

These axioms and the teachings about them were known as the 'Emerald Tablet of Hermes Trismegistus.' He was the mythical figure at the heart of the Hermetic tradition going back to pre-Christian, Babylonian and Egyptian astronomers, astrologers and mystics who had perceived that all things on earth were connected to all things in the heavens and vice versa. They had also perceived that all things celestial converge at the celestial pole, the way to which exoterically is directed by the seven stars of the Great Bear and esoterically by the *visio smaragdus* of the goddess Artemis and her son Arcas-Arthur. There was really no need for Geoffrey of Monmouth to have ever met Adelard. He only needed to have known about his emerald ring and to have understood its meaning.

Cracking the hermetic code

Seen in the mystic light of Adelard's Sufi Emerald stone, which we have now identified as the *smaragdus* of Artemis and her hero son Arcas-Arcturus-Arthur, it isn't hard to interpret Geoffrey's story of the birth of

Fig.13 Map of Almoravid and Seljuk expansion c. 1100

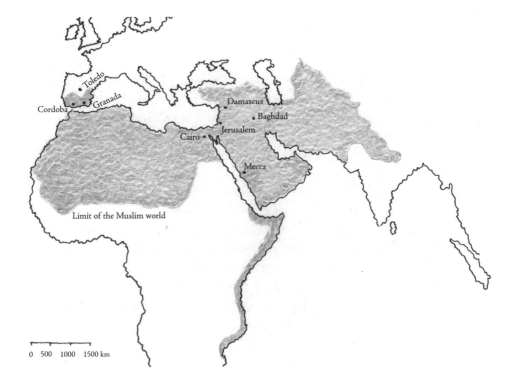

Arthur through the magic of Merlin in Hermetic terms. It is Hermetic star lore, a metaphor, for the rediscovery of the ancient wisdom of the celestial North, which lay behind the geographical north; the North behind the north. It had been known for millennia but had been forgotten because it had been rejected and suppressed by the Christian Church, who had condemned it as pagan as it became increasingly intolerant of any pre-Christian wisdom apart from the Jewish Old Testament. It was almost inevitable that this ancient wisdom could only return to Britain through the Hermetic influence of the Sufis because, unlike the Christian church, Islam had been open to all the subjects embraced by the Greek, Egyptian and Persian civilizations, which they conquered. Astronomy, astrology and alchemy were no exception and were positively encouraged by the Sufis. However, this did not mean that it was essentially Islamic by nature. Islam had fostered it but it all derived from wisdom which predated Islam and Christianity by millennia. Recent research has shown that it was most probably encoded in the alignments of the megalithic stone circles of 3000 to 2000 BC. It could in fact be called an Older Testament because it was centred round Goddess religion, which predated the patriarchy of the Abrahamic faiths. It was only as a by-product of the Crusades and the proto-crusades in Spain and Italy of the eleventh century, as distilled in the Hermetic wisdom, that it was able to percolate through the doctrinal taboos of the church. It was in essence heretical because it was heterodox, was associated with the enemy who were perceived as 'the Infidel' and was deeply astrological. It had, therefore, to be dressed up in code; in stories which have gripped the imagination from the twelfth to the twenty-first century, but which have remained largely misunderstood because, even after eight centuries, the same taboos still remain. Even in our largely post-Christian society, most people today are as ignorant of the Sufis as they ever were and deeply suspicious of astrology. Many still regard Islam as the enemy, as mostly barbarous fundamentalists and terrorists. In fact the current 'war against terrorism' is generally perceived as a war against Islam and some believe that the wars against Afghanistan and Iraq are crusades similar to those in the twelfth century. So, incredible though it may seem, the conditions which gave rise to the Arthurian, Merlin and Grail stories are almost the same today as they were all those centuries ago, and a deeper awareness of the ancient star lore, which they symbolize, is as rare as it ever was.

Geoffrey of Monmouth did not mention the Round Table in his stories but other writers who developed them soon did. The first of these was the

Fig.14 A fourteenth-century illustration of The Story of Lancelot *showing the Knights of the Round Table and a vision of the Holy Grail*

Frenchman, Wace, in *Roman de Brut* in 1155, who said that it came as Guinevere's dowry. It was made by Merlin at the command of Arthur's father, Uther Pendragon, and that it was made 'round in the likeness of the world.'[15] It could seat one hundred and fifty knights and none seemed higher than the rest. This is a thinly disguised reference to the zodiac, which becomes more obvious in the writings of Robert de Boron around 1200. Here the knights or peers are specified as only being twelve: 'The twelve peers of my court will sit in the twelve seats.'[16]

The theme of the Grail was added to Geoffrey's corpus even later than Wace's Round Table. In the mid-1180s it was introduced to an intrigued readership as a mysterious, ambiguous artifact by Chrétien de Troyes in *Perceval,* and was developed from that story by other anonymous authors in the 1180s and 1190s, such as *Perlesvaus* and *The Quest of the Holy Grail.* But it was only in the story of *Joseph of Arimathea* by Robert de Boron that it received clear definition as the cup which Jesus used at the Last Supper. It could be claimed that, as such, it was a straight mainstream transplant from Christianity, which belies any heterodox or Hermetic influence, but this is not the case. Robert de Boron's sources are believed to have been *The Acts of Pilate* and *The Gospel of Nicodemus,* both of which were lost apocryphal Gospels thought to have been brought back from the Crusades and not recognized by the church. In his retelling of the Joseph of Arimathea story, Robert de Boron makes out that the cup of the Last Supper was given to Joseph by the risen Jesus as a present and that, eventually, it was brought by him and his family to Avalon in the west country of Britain. This touched on the old belief, dismissed by the church as legend, that it had originally come from Avalon-Glastonbury and that Jesus had visited Britain as a boy. So although the Grail for Robert appeared to be orthodox, its story was embellished with so many unorthodox presuppositions that it was regarded merely as apocryphal heresy and has remained so down the centuries.[17]

Returning to Geoffrey of Monmouth's original telling of the Merlin stories, there is only one to which it might be hard to give a Hermetic interpretation. This is the famous one in which the boy seer discovers the dragons fighting deep down beneath Vortigern's tower, and which are stopping the building being completed. Yet this story too can be reasonably interpreted as a metaphor for the Caduceus of Hermes, his magic rod embellished with the two intertwined snakes. The Caduceus was the staff, given to Hermes by Apollo and is traditionally the symbol of the two forces of the universe which are ultimately to be united. They are the two serpents of illness and health, hermetic and homeopathic 'nature can overcome nature,' *solve et coagula,* the Alchemical male sulphur and female quicksilver. The wand itself is the *axis mundi,* the axle of the universe mentioned above, up and down which all mediator-messenger gods travel between heaven and earth.

Applying this interpretation to the Merlin story, the fighting dragons can be seen as a metaphor for the agitation set up within the energies of the earth by the fact that a quisling king, on behalf of an alien, invading nation, is attempting to usurp the rulership of the land from Mercury-Hermes. To carry this into history, we would say that the strife caused in Britain by first the invasion of alien Angles and Saxons and later Normans, has been a continuing feature of British history. To this day it could be claimed that the true Hermetic rulership of the land has been

Fig.15 Merlin's revelation of the red and white dragons to King Vortigern

usurped by those ruling as incomers on behalf of another, less spiritual energy. The reign of the Normans and their heirs, based on a hierarchical model, has led to imperial, world greatness but only at the expense of the soul and the esoteric spirit of the land. But the usurpation of the Hermetic spirit extends today far beyond national or racial boundaries. It is now global in as much as the caduceus, as a symbol of the universal magnetic hermetic field, is sadly weakened. Even the semblance of an attempted harmony with nature has been abandoned in favour of an overwhelming belief in material economic growth at the expense of environmental domination and destruction.

The return of the Merlinesque

If the stories of Merlin, Arthur, the Round Table and the Grail can all be reasonably understood as code for the revival of Hermetic star lore in the midst of a largely alien twelfth-century Christian context, then an important question still needs to be addressed: Why did it all come alive in the decades which followed the publication of Geoffrey of Monmouth's history in 1176? The answer up to a point is that at this time the Hermetic writings were becoming known in the West through the travels and scholarship of people such as Adelard of Bath.

However, were there other factors, cosmic factors, which precipitated this great flowering of the manifestations of the axiom of the Emerald Tablet 'As above, so below?' What was going on in the heavens at that time? Could it perhaps have been the position of Arcturus-Arthur in the zodiac at that significant moment in history? It seems possible because, according to the astrological computer program, *Solar Fire,* Arcturus could be found at 12° Libra for most of the twelfth century. Being a 'fixed star' it moves very slowly. It went into 12° Libra in 1130 and on to 13° in 1193. Thus in 1136, the date of Geoffrey of Monmouth's publication, it had just entered 12° Libra. It is remarkable that on Charles Carter's zodiac of epochs in which 1° equals six years, 1136 corresponds to 9.3° Libra, while 12° Libra takes us to 1152. Since a 2° 'orb' of latitude is allowed for an exact conjunction, this may be taken as such. In fact this is so nearly precise that it raises the deeper question concerning the nature of the reality with which we are dealing in Charles Carter's historical zodiac. However, we will leave that for the time being and instead look at another more obvious synchronicity, which might also be the 'as above' corollary of the 'so below' flowering of the Merlin, Arthur and Grail stories.

This other important 'as above' phenomenon, which could be seen as the inspiration for all these 'below' stories could have been the exact conjunction of the planets Uranus and Neptune in 1136. These two outer planets were only discovered in 1781 and 1846 respectively, but that doesn't mean that their effects weren't felt in earlier times. They are only conjunct once every 171 years so their conjunction at the precise date of the publication of Geoffrey of Monmouth's *History,* which saw the 'birth' of Merlin and Arthur is very remarkable. This is taken as more than a coincidence by Richard Tarnas, a well known astrologer and philosopher who, in *Prometheus the Awakener,* comes to the conclusion that the Uranus-Neptune combination is associated in history and personal biographies with: 'periods in which the archetypal — the mythic, the spiritual, the transcendent, the imaginal, the numinous — is suddenly awakened and liberated in new ways into human consciousness.'[19]

According to Tarnas we are in such a period today as a result of the Uranus-Neptune conjunction of 1993. He states that one of the impulses, which it brings with it is a growth in the desire to overcome traditional dualisms between 'human beings and nature, between spirit and matter, mind and body, subject and object, intellect and soul and masculine and feminine.'[20] It is remarkable that his list is so reminiscent of those associated with Hermes' Caduceus! He also lists the upsurge of mystical and out-of-body experiences, which is also attributed to the Uranus-Neptune conjunction. These, in their own way, are comparable to those associated with the twelfth-century Sufis, which featured the Great Bear, the cosmic pole and the emerald light. Although he doesn't list Gandalf, Obi wan Kenobi or Dumbledore, it seems clear to me that he could easily have done so and that we are in the midst of a resurgence of Merlinesque magicians, who together with their equivalent cosmic Arthurs, are enjoying enormous popularity in contemporary imagination, similar to that enjoyed by Merlin, Arthur and the knights of the Round Table in the decades following their initial 'birth' in 1136. However, the most extraordinary coincidence in all this is that the conjunction of Uranus and Neptune in 1136 was in Libra at precisely 12.5°, while, as noted above, Arcturus was at 12° Libra from 1130 to 1193, and was at 12.5° around mid-century! It would seem almost beyond doubt that the cycles of these Uranus-Neptune conjunctions, initially augmented by Arcturus, are still powering these archetypes and have suddenly awakened 'the imaginal and the numinous' Merlinesque and Arthurian myths for our time. In this sense we could say that Merlin and Arthur have returned in other guises.

*Fig.16 Merlin draws a mysterious symbol on King Arthur's shield
(Gustave Doré, nineteenth century)*

3. Arthur's Merlin and Merlin's Arthur

Judging by the popularity of the films *Indiana Jones and the Last Crusade* and *Monty Python and the Holy Grail,* it would seem as though the fascination with the Holy Grail is as great as it ever was historically. Indeed, the phenomenal popularity of *The Da Vinci Code* indicates that, whatever it is understood to have been, the Grail still has the power to grip the imagination of young and old. As many believe, Dan Brown based many of his ideas for his novel on *The Holy Blood and the Holy Grail* by Michael Baigent, Richard Leigh and Henry Lincoln published in 1982. The main theme of their controversial historical research was that the Grail romances of the twelfth and thirteenth centuries, were coded stories about the descendants of the Merovingian Frankish kings in the fifth and early sixth centuries, who were descended from the children born of the secret marriage between Jesus and Mary Magdalene. The heart of their thesis was that the cup of the Last Supper, the *San Greal,* was not a cup at all but a mistranslation of *Sang Réal,* the Royal or Holy Blood:

> In many of the earlier manuscripts, the Grail is called the 'Sangraal;' and even in the later version by Malory, it is called the 'Sangreal.' It is likely that some such form — 'Sangraal' or 'Sangreal' — was in fact the original one. It is also likely that the one word was subsequently broken in the wrong place. In other words 'Sangraal' or 'Sangreal' may not have been intended to divide into 'San Graal' or 'San Greal' — but into 'Sang Raal' or 'Sang Réal.' Or, to employ the modern spelling, Sang Royal, Royal blood.[21]

Baigent, Leigh and Lincoln launched an explosively controversial best seller on an unsuspecting world. Their research into the byways of French history, the Templars, the Cathars, the Gnostics and the mysterious Priory of Sion led a vast, and largely ignorant, readership into an alternative interpretation of the development of Western Christianity, which bewildered, shocked and intrigued them. Dan Brown has taken up these ideas and written a compulsive thriller in which most readers cannot tell the difference between what portends to be historical fact and what is fiction. Meanwhile, many books have been published which seek to crack *The Da Vinci Code* and attempt to educate readers in orthodox Christian truth and, more importantly, heresy.

The extraordinary success of *The Holy Blood and the Holy Grail* as well as Dan Brown's novel has, I believe, been due to the ignorance of most people about the difference between orthodox and heretical Christianity, combined with a general suspicion about the historical churches, especially Roman Catholicism. Most people today, and that includes church people, suspect that, to a greater or lesser extent, the churches have manipulated historical facts to suit themselves. We live in a time of spiritual de-regulation where more and more people are using their freedom to think their own spiritual thoughts and don't want to be told what they should believe by the organized, traditional churches. It is also a time when, thanks to the influence of feminism and the Women's Movement, it is no longer considered sacrilegious to believe that Jesus might have been married and had a family.

Nevertheless, the fact remains that the belief, or rather the speculation, that the Holy Grail might have been the womb of Mary Magdalene, is unique in history. It has never been interpreted that way before. Whatever we may think about it, it must be given full marks for originality, imagination and sheer cheek!

Traditionally, the Grail has always been associated with a cup or dish. The word itself comes from the Latin *gradale* (by degree), and was used to denote a dish, which was brought to the table at the different servings during a meal. The rise in importance of the word in this context was due to Chrétien de Troyes in his famous *Conte del Graal,* written in the 1180s, where he describes the youthful Perceval seated on a couch, eating next to the Fisher King and witnessing a mysterious procession. At each course of the meal this procession of strange symbols passes by in the midst of which is a beautiful woman who holds a jewel-encrusted dish, or *graal,* in her hands. It was fifteen years later that Robert de Boron took this enigmatic dish and turned it into the cup of the Last Supper.[22]

However different this traditional understanding of the Grail is to contemporary, sensational speculation regarding the Holy Bloodline of Jesus and Mary Magdalene, both theories have one important thing in common. They are both about the feminine. For the cup, or chalice, whether seen symbolically as the cornucopia, the horn of plenty or the Celtic cauldron of wisdom, is always interpreted as a feminine symbol in contrast to the masculine blade, spear or lance. When we turn to the Grail as understood in star lore this becomes apparent.

In the last chapter it was demonstrated that the twelfth-century stories about Merlin, Arthur, the Round Table and the Grail, could all be interpreted by means of the Hermetic axiom 'As above, so below.' By so doing it was possible to see it all as meaningful star lore. This hermetic interpretative procedure may not be as sensational as attempting to crack *The Da Vinci Code,* but in its own way it may be just as disturbing and controversial. For while it is most shocking to bring sex into the story of Jesus, it is almost as taboo to take astrology seriously. However, it has been shown already that such a method of interpretation leads to unexpectedly rewarding insights. I believe that, if we explore further, this will continue to be the case.

Charles Carter, it would seem, failed to develop the potential of his theory of Piscean epochs. Maybe he was too distinguished an astrologer to view his theory as professionally respectable. Maybe he was too modest. For whatever reason he missed making certain simple connections which, had he done so, would have perhaps convinced him that he had stumbled on to an ancient and important zodiacal system. I have called it 'the Zodiac of the Grail' because not being either a distinguished or a professional astrologer, I feel that it has about it a certain magic.

The zodiac of the Grail

From the dawn of civilization and in many cultures, as well as in star mythology, the cup of the Last Supper, the Holy Grail, along with magic cauldrons, pots and cups, has been associated with the constellation Alpha Crater (the cup), named after its brightest star, Alkes (or Al-Ka's in Arabic), and is found in the second decanate of Leo. Vivian Robson's summary of its traditional meanings explains:

Magic cauldrons appear in many myths as the purveyors of transformation, and under the guise of cauldrons, pots, chalices, cups, which contain ambrosia or the nectar of life or immortality, or the elixir of the gods. The 'cauldron of plenty' provided an inexhaustible supply of food and was also a source of knowledge and wisdom and the symbol of the fountain of youth. The contents of the Cup are figuratively, the essence distilled from experience, whether joyous or sorrowful. The Holy Grail, Jesus Christ's cup, is associated with this cup; according to medieval legend, the cup said to be used by Jesus Christ at the Last Supper, and by Joseph of Arimathea to collect his blood and sweat at the Crucifixion. It was sought after by medieval knights. Some have associated the contents with sperm and the Cup being related to the womb.[23]

The name of this constellation, Crater, comes from the Greek and its exact spelling is *krateria,* and the first touch of magic we encounter with it is that its hermetic numbers are 540 and 90. The Pythagorean system of assigning numbers to the letters of the alphabet was integral to the Hermetic Corpus, and can be easily explained by listing the individual letters with their equivalent numbers:

K(20) R(100) A(1) T(300) E(8) R(100) I(10) A(1). This adds up to 540.

It is strange that 540 has a strong connection with the Age of Pisces, indeed with all cosmic Ages if they are each taken to last for 2160 years. For 540, if taken as years is exactly one quarter of the total cycle of 2160. This means that we can use it to identify the four cardinal points in Charles Carter's zodiac as we have already been using them. These are the four zero points of the four cardinal signs — 540 Cancer, 1080 Libra, 1620 Capricorn and 2160/0 Aries.

Each word, according to the Pythagorean system, has two numbers. The first, as above, is derived from the well-known system of number-letter equivalence, in which the numbers after 10, go up in 10s and after 100 in 100s. This is known as the Greater Canon. The second, less well-known system is called the Lesser Canon and only uses the numbers 1 to 26. If we analyse *krateria* by this other system, we get:

k(11) r(19) a(1) t(21) e(8) r(19) i(10) a(1). This adds up to 90.

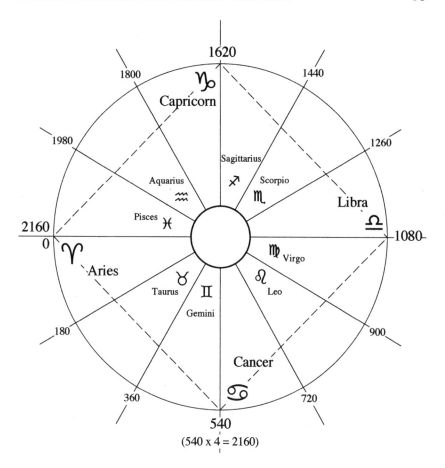

Fig.17 The four cardinal points of the Grail zodiac

Once again it appears to be an odd coincidence that ninety, if again taken as years, is exactly half of one of Carter's epochs of 180 years. Also, if taken as degrees of a 360° circle, it equals a right angle which equates with 540 being a quarter of 2160 according to the other system. Each house of the zodiac represents 30° of the 360° circle, therefore ninety years represent 15°, which is called the mid-point or zenith. It may be compared to midday, when the sun reaches the climax of its daily course. If we go round the twelve epochs and identify their mid-points, we get the following dates:

Aries AD 90, Taurus 270, Gemini 450, Cancer 630, Leo 810, Virgo 990, Libra 1170, Scorpio 1350, Sagittarius 1530, Capricorn 1710, Aquarius 1890 and Pisces 2070.

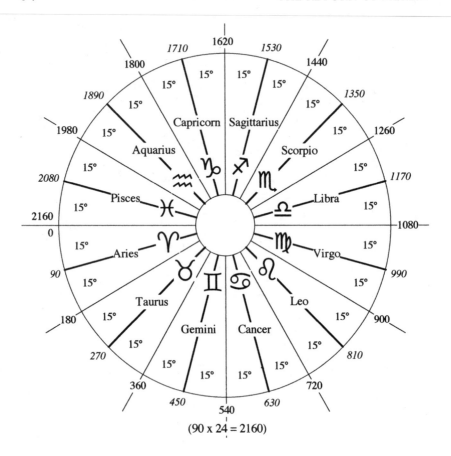

Fig.18 The zenith points of the epochs

So much for the outline description of the zodiac, which can be constructed from the two hermetic or Pythagorean numbers equivalent to *krateria*, the constellation of the Cup.

Charles Carter apparently never saw this connection but then, in fairness, it must be said that he probably didn't know about it and thus was not looking for it. What is perhaps more unexpected and genuinely disappointing, is that he didn't notice the important astrological aspect between the zenith of the epoch during which the main Merlin, Arthurian and Grail romances were written, and the zenith of the epoch during which the protagonists of these romances lived, or were supposed to have lived.

Astrology is all about the exact geometrical angles between individual planets. It is the study of the meaning which can be adduced from these angles. When two planets appear to be together in the sky, they are said to be in conjunction and combine their attributes and powers. When they are 60° apart they are said to be in a sextile relationship. When 90° they are in a right-angled relationship, known to astrologers as a square, when 120° in a trine, when 180° in an opposition. These and other degrees, such as a quintile of 72°, all have their own meaning. One of the hardest aspects is considered to be a square of 90° although in these astrologically correct times it has to be 'challenging.' Similarly, we can no longer call a trine of 120° the very best of aspects because, as we all know, if things come too easily, it just makes us lazy. It is useful to note that trines link zodiac signs of the same element, that is, fire, earth, air and water. However, for those of us who have perhaps discovered that Venus is in a trine relationship with Mars in our own horoscope, the happy relationships we enjoy with the opposite sex will speak for themselves. On the whole we would probably be thankful for it making things too easy than for too much 'challenge' from a square aspect.

The Merlin and Arthur trine

What Charles Carter didn't notice is that the period from Geoffrey of Monmouth to Robert de Boron, 1136 to 1210, is in an exact trine relationship with the Arthurian age, which is usually taken to have started after the Romans left Britain in 410, and to have ended at the Battle of Mount Badon, Arthur's great victory over the Saxons in somewhere around 490–500. If we take the mid-points of Gemini and Libra — 450 and 1170 — this is made clear. Since each sign is a 30° segment of the 360° zodiac circle, it means that a trine, as an angle of 120°, is measured by four signs for $4 \times 30 = 120$.

There are four signs between Gemini and Libra, i.e. Gemini, Cancer, Leo and Virgo. There are, therefore, 120° between 15° Gemini (AD 450) and 15° Libra (AD 1170). This trine is 720 years. 450, for want of detailed historical evidence, could be taken as the date for an early Arthurian victory, and 1170, which saw the start of the romances of Chrétien de Troyes, could be said to be the mid-point of the whole Arthurian-Grail *oeuvre* between Geoffrey of Monmouth and Robert de Boron.

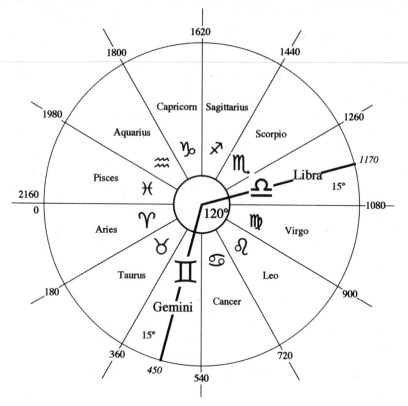

Fig.19 *Trine of the zenith points of Gemini and Libra*

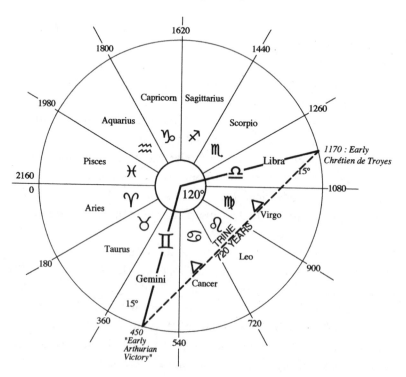

Fig.20 *Trine of 'early Arthurian victory' and early Chrétien de Troyes*

Whatever the astrologically correct may say, the trine relationship is traditionally defined as one of vitality, harmony, equilibrium, ease, beauty, delight, ideals and magnetism. Who can doubt that these felicitous qualities somehow transmitted themselves across the seven centuries of the so called Dark Ages, and then recreated themselves in the early Medieval setting of knighthood, courtly love and the Crusades? How did this happen? There were no computers or data storage facilities in these days. There were scarcely any books. How could it be that it took seven centuries for it to happen, even accepting that the Arthurian and Grail literature was largely the first flowering in Western culture of what we would call the historical novel, and that the post-Roman Britain, about which they wrote, was largely the product of their historical imagination?

Was history repeating itself? Was the Norman conquest of 1066 a repetition of the Anglo-Saxon invasions of the post-Roman period? Under the iron rule of the Norman and Plantagenet invaders, was the only means of dissent possible for the beleaguered spirit of ancient British culture, the romanticized memory of the great stand which Arthur was imagined to have made against the invaders? Is it significant that Geoffrey of Monmouth was Breton, that he wrote his *History* from the point of view of the indigenous Britons, and that his portrayal of Arthur as a great national Celtic hero defeating the Anglo-Saxons was only a thinly disguised tract against the contemporary tyranny of the Normans? This could well be the case, as many commentators have maintained. The dates would certainly fit approximately. Not exactly but within the natural, zodiacal trine formed between the two air signs of Gemini 360 to 540 and Libra 1080 to 1260, for they are 120° or 720 years apart as we have seen.

We could say that history was certainly repeating itself up to a point at least, and that it coincided approximately with the 720 year trine between 15° Gemini in 450 and 15° Libra in 1170. If we made this more precise from 450 to 1066 it would have to be very approximate but would still be within the influence of the general connection between Gemini and Libra, in so much as air signs share the same element which, among other things, is associated with mind, intellect and spirit. There is no point in concocting a theory of history in which the facts are made to fit. This is the usual accusation made against all theories of history, and indeed against most of astrology itself, whose claims to explain human affairs by the stars are usually dismissed as 'coincidences.' However, it

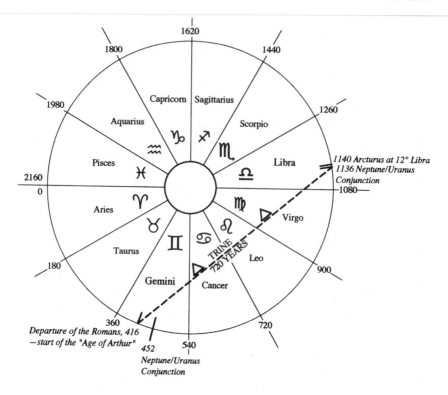

Fig.21 Uranus-Neptune conjunctions in Gemini and Libra

can reasonably be claimed without breaking astrological rules, that even a cycle of 616 years could be considered within the outer cusp, or outer orb of influence, of the energies of these two epochs.

What is remarkable is that, if we return to the thesis of Richard Tarnas, that the conjunction of the planets Uranus and Neptune causes an upsurge of 'the archetypal — the mythic, the spiritual, the transcendent, the imaginal, the numinous' both in personal biographies and the collective, we find that a Uranus-Neptune conjunction took place in AD 452. It was a triple conjunction and took place in the sign of Leo, the king. 452 is almost exactly at the zenith of the epoch of Gemini. This was 684 years before the one in 1136, which we claimed triggered off the 'birth' of Arthur and Merlin in Medieval literature. This brings us closer to a genuine trine relationship, which suggests that the strength of Charles Carter's theory of epochs may lie in the 171 year cycle of Uranus and Neptune conjunctions which would be near enough to the 180 unit to give us the exact 720 (180 × 4) trine.

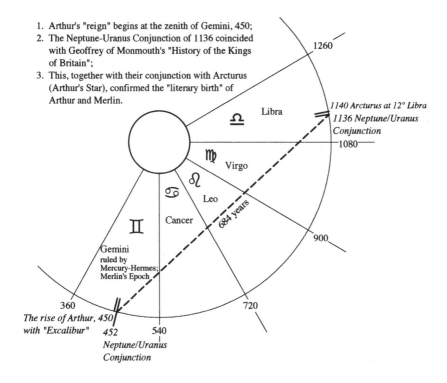

1. Arthur's "reign" begins at the zenith of Gemini, 450;
2. The Neptune-Uranus Conjunction of 1136 coincided with Geoffrey of Monmouth's "History of the Kings of Britain";
3. This, together with their conjunction with Arcturus (Arthur's Star), confirmed the "literary birth" of Arthur and Merlin.

Fig.22 The rise of Arthur with Excalibur

But more important than this to our inquiry into the identity of Merlin and Arthur in star mythology, is the discovery that there was a triple, and thus extremely important, conjunction of Uranus and Neptune in 452 in the sign of Leo. As mentioned, 450 is the zenith of the epoch of Gemini, and Gemini is ruled by Mercury. Mercury is Hermes and one of Hermes' disguises is Merlin. It could, therefore, be claimed that the epoch of Gemini, from 360 to 540, was ruled by Merlin and that the Mercurial-Hermetic energies of that time gave Merlin's magic its particular power. If we consider that the epoch of Gemini *was* Merlin's epoch then 15° of that epoch would be the time of his maximum potency. His 'magic' would have been most effective around 450.

The coincidence with the conjunction of Uranus and Neptune in the sign of Leo is most remarkable because, looking at these events through the lens of hermetic symbols, a heroic kingly figure emerges from the archetypal, imaginal, numinous mists of Merlin. He is the figure of Arthur. It is Arthur who epitomizes the mythology of the Uranus-Neptune

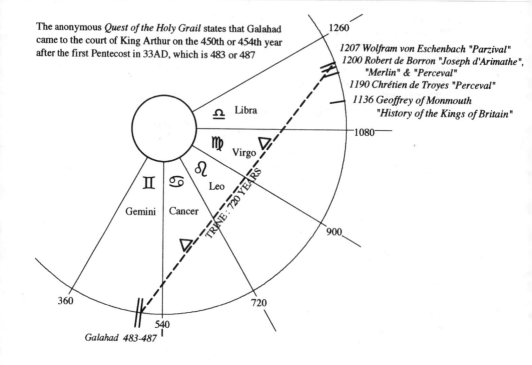

The anonymous *Quest of the Holy Grail* states that Galahad came to the court of King Arthur on the 450th or 454th year after the first Pentecost in 33AD, which is 483 or 487

1260

1207 Wolfram von Eschenbach "Parzival"
1200 Robert de Borron "Joseph d'Arimathe",
"Merlin" & "Perceval"
1190 Chrétien de Troyes "Perceval"
1136 Geoffrey of Monmouth
"History of the Kings of Britain"

1080

Libra

Virgo

Leo

Gemini   Cancer

TRINE: 720 YEARS

900

360

720

540

Galahad 483-487

Fig.23 Galahad and the later literature of the Grail

conjunction in Leo, the sign of kingship. It is Arthur who comes alive as the champion of the ancient British around 450 for that is the zenith of the epoch of Merlin who, as Hermes, is the chthonic (underworld) ruler of Britain and conjures Arthur by his magic as the *dux bellorum* of the goddess Artemis, his mother, who Merlin also serves (see Chapter 4). It is through the power of Excalibur that Arthur restores the sovereignty of the land to his mother Artemis. It is in her guise as the Lady of the Lake that she first fashions Excalibur in her watery workshops. It is through the agency of Merlin that she gives it to Arthur and it is to her that it is returned by Sir Bedevere as Arthur lies dying after the fateful battle in the West. If the date of Arthur's literary 'birth' may be taken as 1136, then the date when he began to restore the rightful sovereignty of the land to the Goddess was 452 at the height of Merlin's magic:

> King Arthur's sword, Excalibur,
> Wrought by the lonely maiden of the Lake

> Nine years she wrought it, sitting in the deeps
> Upon the hidden bases of the hills.[24]

This would agree with the only actual fifth century date given in any of the twelfth-century Grail stories. This, extraordinarily, is given as 450 or 454, when we are told that Galahad came to the Court of King Arthur. It is in the anonymous *Quest of the Holy Grail,* dating from between 1195 and 1230 and thus pin-points the same moment in time which we have identified as the beginning of Arthur's mythological 'reign.'[25] However, it is not such a coincidence as it seems at first, because it says that Galahad came to the court of Arthur at Pentecost and that this was the 454th or 450th Pentecost after the resurrection. Since it does not say that it was from the birth of Christ it means we must add the traditional 33 years for Christ's life which brings us up to 450 + 33 = 483 or 454 + 33 = 487. Since Galahad, as the son of Lancelot, was a second-generation knight of the Round Table, it means that, if Arthur's battles began around 450 then by 483 or 487 the time was ripe for the appearance of the perfect Christian knight. The specifically Christian cavalry had arrived to secure lasting Christian victory!

The interpretation of Arthur as the personification of the extraordinary resurgence of the powers of the northern tribes, fits the historical facts very well. For, as mentioned above, Caesar tells us that the deity they revered most was Mercury, and if there is any 'truth' in Charles Carter's theory of epochs, then the period from 360 to 540 was the time of Mercury's epoch. If Arthur is taken as the collective name for the armies under the banner of Mercury, and if the magic powers of the King-maker are symbolized by Merlin-Mercury, then it all fits. Geoffrey of Monmouth was right after all because, according to this symbolic and collective interpretation, the troops of 'Arthur' *did* conquer Europe and Rome. This would be the symbolic interpretation of the collapse of the Roman Empire under the onslaught of the Northern tribes; the abandonment of Britain in 410; the sacking of Rome under Alaric the Goth in 410; the barbarian settlement of Roman provinces throughout the Empire after 425; Attila the Hun's victories until his death in 453; the destruction of Roman possessions in North Africa by Gaiseric before 443; the sack of Rome again by the Vandals in 455; the destruction of the Roman fleet off Cartagena in 460 and the end of the Western Roman Empire in 476.

This is not history as we know it or teach it today and would be regarded as fictional as Archdeacon Walter's old book in the British language, which Geoffrey of Monmouth claimed to have been his historical source. But it *was* history from the point of view of the hermetic dictum 'As above, so below.' It still in a sense is, in so far as we, the dispossessed children of Hermes, the ancient chthonic ruler of our land, remember 'with advantages' the deeds of our great King Arthur and believe that he will come again to take rightful possession of his, or to be more exact, his mother's land.

The trine to Tennyson's Arthur

In the last chapter it was proposed that the 'As above,' of the hermetic axiom which found its 'so below' equivalence in the literary 'birth' of Merlin and Arthur in Geoffrey of Monmouth's *History* published around 1135–36, was the conjunction of Uranus and Neptune in exactly the same year. This is the conjunction, which Richard Tarnas claims is accompanied by an upsurge of the archetypal, the mystical, the imaginal and the numinous, in the individual and the collective. It was also claimed that while this was in itself enough to give rise to these mythic and archetypal figures, it was the extraordinary coincidence of the conjunction of Arcturus-Arthur's star, with this Uranus-Neptune conjunction in Libra in Charles Carter's zodiac that made these heroic 'births' almost inevitable.

Tracing back a trine (that is, 120° or 720 years), from 1136 to 416, took us to the beginning of the Age of Arthur itself, which is usually presumed to have begun after the Romans left Britain in AD 410. An approximate trine with AD 452 took us to an earlier Uranus-Neptune conjunction in Leo, the house of the king, 684 years earlier. The coincidence of this 452 conjunction with 450 being the zenith or 15° point of Carter's epoch of Gemini, ruled by Mercury who is Hermes, one of whose aliases is Merlin, seemed enough to justify the personification of these energies as 'Arthur,' who with his northern tribes, became victorious over the Roman Empire, which for centuries had usurped the power of the Celtic kingdoms.

Now, if we move *forward* a trine it is remarkable that we find the same pattern emerging. Adopting the same procedure we find that from the mid-point of the epoch of Libra to the-mid point of Aquarius takes us from 1170 to 1890.

**Floris
Books**

Postcard

Floris Books
15 Harrison Gardens
Edinburgh EH11 1SH
UK

Stamp
required

Floris Books

To receive information and special offers on other Floris Books publications, please return this card with your details

Name (BLOCK CAPS): _____

Address: _____

_____

Postcode: _____ Country: _____

Email: _____

if you want to receive information this way

We will never pass on your details to anyone else

☐ Please send me your complete catalogue once

I am interested in receiving regular information on (please tick):

☐A Religion and Spirituality
  ☐AA *Christian Spirituality*
  ☐AB *Bible*
  ☐AC *World Spirituality*
  ☐AD *Celtic Spirituality*
  ☐AE *Science and Spirituality*
☐B Self-Help and Popular Psychology
☐C Mind Body Spirit
  ☐CA *Holistic Health*

☐D Art and Architecture
☐E Language and Literature
☐F Biography
☐G Organics
☐H Philosophy
☐I Steiner Education
  ☐IA *Steiner Teacher Resources*
☐J Child Health and Development

☐K Picture Books
  ☐KA *Elsa Beskow Books*
☐L Activities and Craft
☐M Story Books
☐N Young Fiction
  ☐NA *Flyways*
  ☐NB *Kelpies*

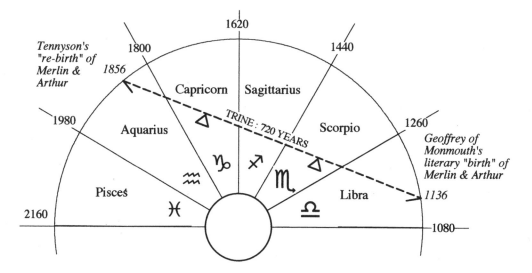

Fig.24 Trine from Geoffrey of Monmouth to Tennyson

However, if we go directly to the exact trine of Arthur and Merlin's literary 'birth,' that is from 1136 to 1856, we encounter a striking phenomenon. For it was at that time exactly that Arthur, Merlin, the Knights and Ladies of the Round Table and the stories of the Grail were all coming alive again and were gripping the popular imagination as never before since their medieval creation — through the poetry of Tennyson.

Tennyson had begun to write on Arthurian themes as early as 1832 with 'The Lady of Shalott.' He had followed in 1842 with 'Sir Launcelot and Queen Guinevere,' 'Sir Galahad,' and 'Morte d'Arthur.' These were not as popular initially as they became later, and the criticism he received hurt him deeply. This was particularly with regard to John Stirling's negative comments on 'Morte d'Arthur' in the *Quarterly Review.* This, more than any of the others, had grieved him because it held great personal significance for him, having been written shortly after the tragic death of his close friend, Arthur Hallam in 1833. The two Arthurs were closely connected in his imagination.

However, during the next decade things changed. The Victorian taste for all things Medieval grew enormously. This was epitomized in 1848 by the formation of the Pre-Raphaelite Brotherhood (the PRB), whose leading members, the artists Dante Gabriel Rossetti, Holman Hunt and

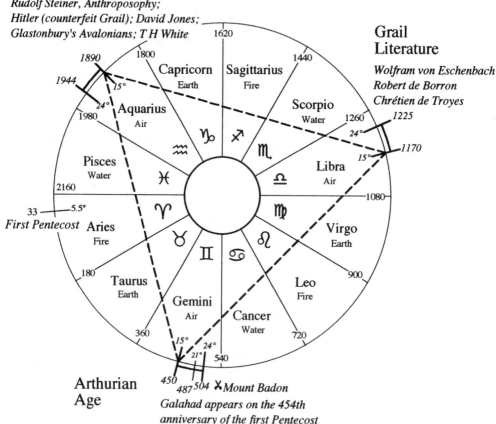

Grail Revival

Tennyson; Pre-Raphaelites;
William Morris; Wagner's Parsifal 1882;
Rudolf Steiner, Anthroposophy;
Hitler (counterfeit Grail); David Jones;
Glastonbury's Avalonians; T H White

Grail Literature

Wolfram von Eschenbach
Robert de Borron
Chrétien de Troyes

Fig.25 The Grail tradition and a grand trine in air signs

John Everett Millais and their friends, pledged themselves to be true to the aesthetic values of the Middle Ages as they believed them to have been, before they had been corrupted by those of the Italian Renaissance after the time of Raphael. After John Ruskin defended them in the London *Times*, their popularity grew enormously.

The revival of the Gothic style in architecture was also becoming fashionable. This was greatly increased when the contract to rebuild the

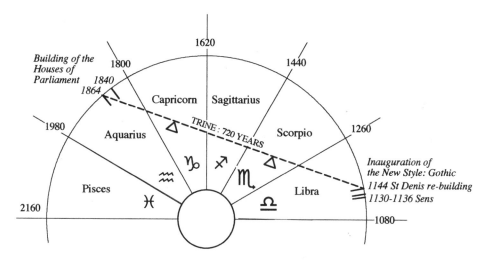

Fig.26 Birth and re-birth of Gothic archictecture

Houses of Parliament went to the great Gothic architect Charles Barry in 1836. When the rebuilding began in 1840, it was as though a new Gothic Age was dawning, even though it was severely criticized by the leading neo-Classicists of the day. Kenneth Clark in *The Gothic Revival* sees this rebuilding as being at a mid-point, pivotal to the development of the movement, between the earlier Picturesque and the later Ethical period. These two periods were both embodied to a spectacular degree in the new Palace of Westminister. Clark writes: 'In time the Houses of Parliament stand midway between the two periods; but in style and general effect they belong to the first. They are a triumph of the Picturesque.'[26] The old buildings had been burnt down in a disastrous fire in 1834 and the rebuilding took place between 1840 and 1864. It is extraordinary that the equivalent dates which trine with those in the twelfth century were 1120 and 1144, for this saw the building of the very first, original cathedral in the 'New Style,' as the Gothic was first called, and was at Sens between 1130 and 1136. Those years also saw the famous renovation of the West End and then the East End of St Denis Abbey by Abbot Suger during the late 1130s and early 1140s, which culminated in the much celebrated national inauguration of the 'New Style' in 1144. This was an *exact trine* of 720 years with 1864, which is truly remarkable.

This trine can be extended into the following years, if we compare the second period of revived Gothic after 1864 in the latter part of the

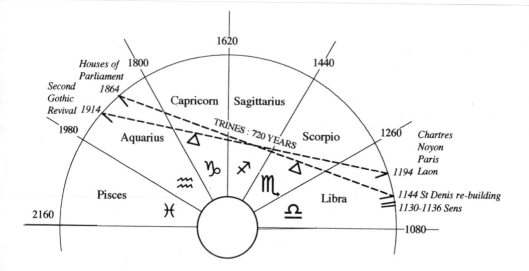

Fig.27 *The Gothic trine extended. There is an extended trine of 720 years between the rise of the Gothic from 1144–94 and the flowering of the Neo-Gothic second, mature, 'ethical' period from 1864–1914.*

nineteenth century, to the years following 1144 which saw the great days of what has been called 'the Cathedrals' Crusade.' For it was during these years that many of the original Gothic cathedrals such as Laon, Paris, Senlis and Noyon were built, culminating with Chartres after 1194.

There is also an almost uncanny continuing trine between the development of the new Tennysonian Grail literature of the nineteenth century and the original Grail Romances from Chrétien de Troyes in the 1170s, to Robert de Boron's corpus of around 1200, and Wolfram von Eschenbach's *Parzival* in 1208.

It was not only the Pre-Raphaelite Brotherhood and the growing fashion for Gothic architecture, which changed the public appreciation of Tennyson. By the time he published the first four of his *Idylls of the King* in 1859 — 'Enid,' 'Elaine,' 'Vivian' and 'Guinevere' — there had been a growing number of Arthurian publications. Noticeable among these were *King Arthur* by Bulwer Lytton in 1848; 'Tristram and Iseult' by Matthew Arnold in 1852; 'Elayne le Blanc,' 'Queen Guinevere' and 'The Parting of Launcelot and Guinevere' by Edward Robert Lytton in 1855, and *The Defence of Guinevere* by William Morris in 1858. Pugin's

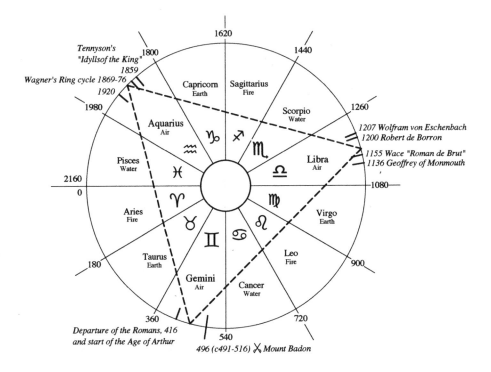

Fig.28 A grand trine exists between the original age of Arthur in the fifth century, the age of Merlin-Arthur and the Grail romances of the twelfth century and the Tennysonian Arthurian epoch of 1859–1920

Contrasts of 1836 and Ruskin's *The Stones of Venice* of 1851 also contributed to these changes.

These and other factors, as Christine Poulson explains in *The Quest for the Grail, Arthurian Legend in British Art 1840 to 1920*, brought about the transformation of attitude to Tennyson's Arthurian poetry. Chief of these other factors was the growing appeal of Tennyson himself. It was after the publication of *In Memoriam* in 1850 that his popularity increased by leaps and bounds. That year he became Poet Laureate and by the time of Prince Albert's untimely death in 1861, which gave *In Memoriam* a national poignancy, he had become the fountainhead and arbiter of national sensibility.

After this an elegiac mood hung over the rest of the Victorian era and we find a Tennysonian nostalgia, melancholy and sadness projected onto many of the artistic illustrations of his Arthurian poems, which proliferated later in the century. Many of these are still well known today and, like Tennyson's poems themselves, still define for us the way in which we picture the Arthurian tales. Despite the enormous changes in artistic fashion, which took over with the Avant Garde after 1870, such as Impressionism, Post-Impressionism, Symbolism and Fauvism followed by the full-blown modernism of Cubism, Expressionism and Abstraction, these Arthurian pictures have retained their appeal. They have been called sentimental, nostalgic, even kitsch, by modernists; nevertheless, they continue to appeal and still are seen in important exhibitions and their reproductions are still sold. In certain circles, it could be claimed, they have come back into fashion. These include *Piety; The Departure of the Knights of the Round Table on the Quest for the Holy Grail* by William Dyce (1849); *The Beguiling of Merlin* by Edward Burne-Jones (1872–77); *Morte d'Arthur* by John Carnick (1862); *The Attainment: The Vision of the Holy Grail to Sir Galahad, Sir Bors and Sir Perceval* by Edward Burne-Jones, William Morris and J.K. Dearle (1890); *The Coming of Arthur* by Joseph West (1894) and *Arthur* by Charles Butler (1904).

It hardly needs stating with all the evidence cited above, that the impact of the outpouring of Tennyson's Arthurian poetry, together with the extraordinary resurgence of neo-Gothic architecture and PRB Medievalism, from the mid-nineteenth century, produced a new Arthurian culture in late Victorian Britain which, in its own way, matched the original age of the Grail romances in the late twelfth and early thirteenth centuries. However, what must be emphasized is that it is extraordinary that all the dates we have examined are in either an exact trine or approximate trine relationship — that is, 720 or 700 years! A pattern has emerged from all these observations which is based on these trines and the trines which emerged earlier for us between these dates in the twelfth century and those in the fifth century in the Age of Arthur himself. When three points in any personal horoscope create trine relationships — that is, in the form of an equilateral triangle — either in the birth chart or in the pattern of transitting planets, this is called a grand trine, and is interpreted by astrologers as a most fortunate configuration; possibly the most fortunate there could be. Even if sceptics would still wish to dismiss all this as coincidence, perhaps they would still have to admit that the combination of all these 'coincidences' is nevertheless really rather extraordinary.

The discovery of Neptune and Uranus

The trines which we have discovered between the revived Arthuriana of Tennyson, the Neo-Gothic revival espoused so passionately by Augustus Pugin, John Ruskin and William Morris, and the PRB on the one hand and their equivalent twelfth-century original prototypes on the other, are so pervasive, so extensive and so persuasive, that we might suspect that there was more to their 'As above' than the 700 to 720 year trines alone. Surely there must have been more of significance going on in the heavens at that time to account for all these cycles repeating themselves so clearly? There was indeed, and the first thing, which must be mentioned, is the Uranus-Neptune conjunction of 1821. Although this was nearly a generation prior to the dramatic rise of the neo-Gothic, the PRB and the early Tennyson Arthurian Romances, it was nevertheless very much the trigger for the Romantic Movement in its earlier manifestations. Richard Tarnas, in the same essay quoted earlier, is in no doubt about this, citing Shelley, Keats and many other great Romantics:

> If we move back to the immediately preceding Uranus-Neptune Conjunction, that of 1815–1829, centred round the year 1821, we find a similar emergence of the archetypal, mythic, transcendent and numinous into the collective psyche with the great age of Romanticism at its height. Here was Shelley, reading Plato at sea and writing *Prometheus Unbound,* seeking to combine the ideal spiritual realm with a revolution in consciousness bringing new freedom to humanity. Here was Keats writing his great odes, beginning with 'On First Looking into Chapman's Homer' (where he compares his awakening to the numinous mythic realm to the discovery of Uranus: 'Then felt I like a watcher of the skies ...'). Here were Byron, Schubert, Stendhal, Scott, as well as Coleridge working out a profound Romantic philosophical perspective in his *Biographia Literaria;* Goethe and Beethoven in their inspired culminating years ... And here was the great wave of births of individuals whose extraordinary imaginative visions would so enrich world literature in the nineteenth century — Dostoevsky, Tolstoy, Melville, Flaubert, Turgenev, the Brontës, George Eliot, Baudelaire, Whitman.[27]

Admittedly, the period of this Uranus-Neptune conjunction, 1815–29 was considerably before our rash of PRB, Gothic and Arthurian trines, yet to students of the Romantic Movement, the period of the High Romantic and that of the Later Romantics can nevertheless still be seen as parts of the development of the one Romantic process. Tarnas would not have to stretch the limits of his generation of creative Uranus-Neptune geniuses at all in order to include Augustus Pugin born in 1812, John Ruskin born in 1819 or Tennyson himself, born 1809. He could easily, and indeed should, have included them all. Even the PRB leaders Rossetti, Hunt and Millais, all born by 1830, come within its range.

However, it is not necessary to stretch the influence of the Uranus-Neptune conjunction too far, for there was another important event in the heavens which gave the mythic and the numinous a great mid-century boost and brought the energies of mysticism and particularly psychic experiences into public consciousness in a new and dramatic way. This important event was the discovery of the planet Neptune itself in 1846.

When a new planet is discovered, astrologers understand that it manifests its distinctive qualities in the events which are occurring at the time, and which reflect these qualities in subsequent years. It is as if the planet is responding to its having been discovered by allowing its influence to be felt in ways characteristic of its arrival into human consciousness. One of the ways in which this new Neptunian consciousness is believed to have become manifest, was in the rise in the occurrence of psychic experiences. It was at this time that seances began and psychic mediums developed their powers to put people in touch with departed spirits 'on the other side.' As Charles Carter notes regarding the discovery of Neptune in the postscript to his essay, *Newly Discovered Planets;* 'Spiritualism in its modern form began with the alleged phenomena of the Fox Sisters in 1848.'

I believe that it was this discovery of Neptune, in 1846, which gave the High Romantic period an extra lease of life. It prolonged the period during which the extreme rationalism of the Enlightenment and the materialism of the rise of the British commercial empire, could be resisted, or at least juxtaposed by the sense of the mysteriousness of the Universe and by the unfathomableness of experiences which were giving a new meaning and soul to life and to society. In art, it was brilliantly expressed in the growth of fairy paintings

• the discovery of Uranus in 1781,
• the start of the epoch of Aquarius, ruled by Uranus, in 1800,
• 10° Aquarius in 1850,
• the Uranus-Neptune conjunction in 1821,
• the discovery of Neptune in 1846, and
• the Uranus-Pluto conjunction in 1850-51

all helped to enhance the archetypal, mythic, numinous Trine with the Age of the Grail Romances in Libra

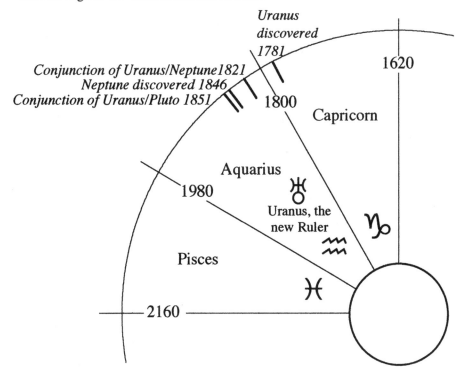

Fig.29 Enter Uranus and Neptune

around that time, but would almost completely explain the rapid rise of the PRB, the Gothic Revival and the 'return' of Arthur in the following years.

I believe that the impact of the discovery of Neptune was doubly profound in the years following its discovery because it took place during the epoch of Aquarius. Uranus had also been discovered in

1781 and its discovery is usually held to have been the agent which triggered off first the American revolution in 1776 and then the French Revolution in 1789. Its discovery thus hastened the arrival of the epoch of Aquarius itself which according to Carter, started in 1800. This was because Uranus had been assigned by astrologers to the new rulership of Aquarius. Thus we can assume that with the forces of Aquarius being so strong anyway and, having recently been greatly strengthened by the Uranus-Neptune conjunction in 1821, it would not have taken much for a sudden increase of Neptunian influence, caused by its discovery, to precipitate forces which would strongly resemble those of a Uranus-Neptune conjunction.

By 1846–50 the epoch of Aquarius, with its new Uranian rulership, had reached 10°, and this angle, as in any zodiacal month, is known to be when the forces associated with that month seriously set in. For instance, the 10° point in Scorpio manifests as the ghostly power of Hallowe'en, the old Samhain; the 10° point of Taurus manifests the celebrations of May Day, or the old Beltane; and strangely enough the 10° point of Aquarius traditionally manifests as the celebration of new birth at Candlemas, or St Bride, the old Imbolc. So we could say that by 1848 at 9.5° of Aquarius, the Uranian forces of St Bride-Imbolc had definitely been established and had set off the equivalent of a Uranus-Neptune conjunction which manifested itself in the PRB, the Gothic revival and, most importantly for us, the return of Arthur, Merlin, the Knights and Ladies of the Round Table and the Quest for the Holy Grail.

Without getting too complicated, it perhaps would be necessary to add to all these 'As above' phenomena, the triple conjunction between Uranus and Pluto in 1850–51 which Richard Tarnas sees as highly influential at this time, although more with the political revolutions around Europe in 1848, than with specifically cultural events. This may not seem directly relevant to our theme, but nevertheless these 1848 revolutions, which took place almost simultaneously throughout Europe, can be interpreted as the upsurge of a general movement towards democracy and, thus, in our mythological terms, towards the establishment of the Round Table at which 'no man could boast that he was exalted above his fellow.' In fact, we perhaps could legitimately add, that this was a movement towards the trine with the original Round Table, made by Merlin and given to Guinevere at her wedding to Arthur. This powerful myth, as we explained earlier, was contrived by Wace the Frenchman who developed Geoffrey of Monmouth's stories in 1160. Its trine came in 1880 by which time the political development of Europe had moved substantially closer to democracy.

The Uranus-Neptune conjunction of 1821, the discovery of Neptune in 1846, the increased Uranian energies born of the discovery of Uranus in 1781, and its influence on the whole period as a result of its newly appointed rulership of the epoch of Aquarius, all combined to strengthen the impact of the Medieval Arthurian trine between the 'birth' of Arthur and Merlin at the pen of Geoffrey of Monmouth in 1136, and their 'rebirth' at the pen of Alfred Lord Tennyson. The combination of all these factors produced a creative, mytho-poetic *oeuvre,* which was so powerful and so sustained that it, to some extent at least, is still with us today.

The great counterfeit Grail deception

At the risk of reading too much into the impact of the movements of Uranus and Neptune on the archetypal, mystical, numinous and especially psychic developments of the nineteenth century, it is nevertheless legitimate to outline a negative story, which seems to have arisen as the expression of the darker qualities also associated with Neptune; namely illusion and deception. It also seems to have been aided by the conjunction of Neptune with Pluto in 1891. This is the rarest of the conjunctions of the outer planets and only occurs once every 492 years. As a result, it has been difficult for astrologers to fully assess its impact. Pluto was discovered in 1930 and is associated with the rise of fascism in the 1930s, and it would seem that there was a link between the inception of what became the Nazi party in the 1890s and its rise to power in the German National Socialist movement during the 1930s. We can almost sense the purer archetypal expression of the Arthurian and Grail motif, which as we have seen arose out of the Uranus-Neptune relationship being, first undermined and then traduced by the growing relationship between the deceptive, illusory aspect of Neptune and the darkly destructive aspect of the traditional god of the underworld, Pluto. In a most powerful way the music of Wagner perfectly expressed both these themes; the more idealistic and redemptive

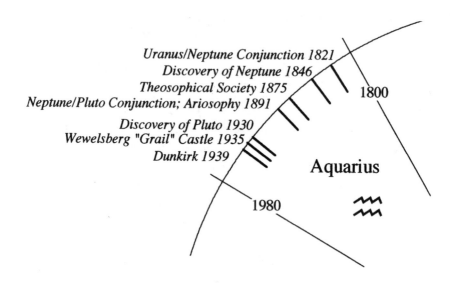

Fig.30 The rise of the counterfeit Grail

Uranus-Neptune relationship in *Lohengrin* written significantly during the time of the discovery of Neptune in 1846 to 1848, also in *Tristan and Isolde* in 1857 and supremely in *Parsifal* written between 1877 and 1882. The darker and more deceptive Neptune-Pluto energies were expressed in the four operas of his *Der Ring des Nibelungen,* completed in 1876. This was based on the medieval German saga of the *Nibelungenlied* originally composed, strangely, around 1200 at almost the exact time of the Grail romances of Robert de Boron and Wolfram von Eschenbach. As is well known, the music of Wagner was endorsed by the Nazi party and was closely associated with its rise and indeed its fall. But here the distinction must be made between the theme of the Grail and that of *The Ring,* between that which seemed to reflect the positive idealism of the Uranus-Neptune relationship and that which seemed, with equal power, to reflect the darkness and deception of the Neptune-Pluto relationship.

It might appear to be a far-fetched analysis of the reasons for the defeat of Hitler in 1945 by the Allied Troops, to say that by choosing the Neptune-Pluto path of *The Ring,* Hitler's fall came almost as a self-fulfilling prophecy in so much as, modelled on the fall of the *Nibelungenlied* hero Siegfried, it could only end in the catastrophe of Götterdämmerung, the Twilight of the Gods. This is so obvious that, had we been living in the time of the Old Testament prophets we might perhaps have been tempted to claim that 'the stars in their courses fought against' Hitler. Strangely, it has been said that Winston Churchill was secretly advised during the war by a well-known political astrologer and that that astrologer was none other than our own Charles Carter! Yet again it seems strangely relevant to recall that the essay in which he explained his theory of Piscean epochs was published shortly after the Second War in a slim volume called *An Introduction to Political Astrology.* Who knows, perhaps he advised Churchill that the power of the ongoing Uranus-Neptune relationship would prevail over that of Neptune-Pluto.

Quite apart from this speculation, however, it must be noted that for many years now, the association of Hitler and leading members of the Nazi party, with the darker side of the late nineteenth-century occult movements, has been known and documented. In popular books such as *Occult Reich* by J.H. Brennan, and scholarly works such as *The Occult Roots of Nazism* by Nicholas Goodrich-Clarke, overwhelming evidence is presented for interpreting the whole Nazi phenomenon in occult terms. An outline of their researches takes us back to the influence of Neptune after its discovery in 1848, and the foundation of the international Theosophical Society in 1875. This was a very Neptunian expression of mystical pluralism, inspired by the syncretistic writings of the Russian psychic, Madam Blavatsky, whose first book, *Isis Unveiled,* caused a sensation throughout the Anglo-Saxon world. The new psychic culture, which rose around her and the Theosophical Society in the 1880s, included mediumship, seances and the study of ancient magical practices as noted earlier. It was mainly healthy and sane, but it also contained aspects which were spiritually suspect or even sinister.

Among the latter were the Order of New Templars and the Thule Society, both of which distorted the mystical pluralism of Theosophy and changed it into the Ariosophy of the Master Race. Hitler, and many of those who later became leaders of the Nazi party, had associations with, or were members of, these groups and fed off the pan-Germanism they preached, which was based on the writings of Guido von List (1848–1919) and Jorg Lanz von Liebenfels (1874–1954).

The Ariosophists mixed folk nationalism and Aryan racism with occultism to support their belief in German world rule. Although they were only marginally active in practical politics, their ideas and symbols

filtered through to the national racist groups associated with the early
Nazi party and, in time, exerted a strong influence on Himmler's SS.
Ariosophical doctrines mixed elitist theories derived from Gnosticism,
Social Darwinism and Eastern gurus, such as Gurdjieff, to revive the
spirit of the medieval German Teutonic Knights. In Himmler's SS
this had strong overtones of the military prowess of the knights of the
Holy Grail as interpreted through the inspiration of Wagner's operas,
especially *The Ring Cycle, Tristan and Isolde* and *Lohengrin.* The
story is long and complex but I believe it gives the clue which enables
us to see the whole rise of this powerful tyranny as a counterfeit Grail
movement, in which the more benign energies of the Uranus-Neptune
relationship had been usurped by the more malign side of the Neptune-
Pluto relationship. If I were to choose an event to epitomize this, it
would be the placing of Wewelsburg Castle under the direct control
of Himmler in February 1935. This was his counterfeit Grail Castle in
which, like a latter-day Klingsor, he and his henchmen could attempt
to weave black magic over their operations. Nicholas Goodrich-Clarke
tells the story:

> The development of the Wewelsburg near Paderborn as
> the SS order-castle and ceremonial centre must represent
> Weishor's most spectacular contribution to the Third
> Reich. During the Nazi electoral campaign of January
> 1933, Himmler travelled through Westphalia, making
> his first acquaintance with the 'land of Hermann and the
> Widukund,' the mythical atmosphere of the Teutoburger
> Forest, a drive up to the Hermannsdenkmal in fog, and
> the romantic Grevensburg Castle, where the Führer's
> party stayed overnight, impressed Himmler deeply and
> made him think of acquiring a castle in this area for SS
> purposes. After two other castles had been considered in
> the course of the year, Himmler viewed the Wewelsburg
> with members of his personal staff on 3rd November
> 1933 and made his choice that very evening. After a fur-
> ther visit in April, the castle was officially taken over by
> the SS in August 1935. The Wewelsburg began its new
> career as a museum and SS officers' college for ideo-
> logical education within the Race and Settlement Main
> Office, but was then placed under the direct control of

the Reichsführer-SS Personal Staff in February 1935. This transfer reflected the increasing importance of the castle to Himmler and the germination of his plans for an SS order-castle, comparable to the Marienburg of the Medieval Teutonic knights.[28]

It may seem an eccentric way of analyzing the nature of the forces which came into such violent opposition during World War Two but looking at the outline of the rise of Ariosophy as a racist splinter group from Theosophy in the late nineteenth century and the influence it had on the rise of early Nazism, helps us to realize to what extent occult ideology had set the scene generations before. In that sense it is not unreasonable to juxtapose the forces of Neptune-Pluto against those of Uranus-Neptune. By the logic of the Hermetic dictum 'As above, so below' it would seem highly reasonable. Added to this, the fact that 1920 saw the almost exact trine both with the *Nibelungenlied* which inspired Wagner's *Ring Cycle,* and with Wolfram von Eschenbach's *Parzival* which inspired his Christian Grail opera of the same name, enables us to see the opposing armies as representing a great Battle of the trines, 720 years on. Going back another 720 years we come to the year 580 which was the period prior to Arthur's famous victory over the invading Saxons at Mons Badonius, Mount Badon, which is thought to have taken place around 590. Was history repeating itself twice over at intervals of approximately 720 years, or are these cycles, like the qualities of Neptune, illusory and deceptive and like those of Pluto racist and politically incorrect?

To make a more positive assessment the striking grand trine between these three auspicious moments of Arthurian history could perhaps allow us to invoke the spirit of Arthur himself. Perhaps he had come alive again in the rhetoric and leadership of Churchill in the pre-war and early war years. Perhaps Merlin was once again on hand to weave his magic and create adverse weather conditions to stop Hitler invading in 1940 and dead calm for the evacuation of Dunkirk in 1939. Perhaps we had forgotten that in Tennyson's *Morte d'Arthur,* Arthur never actually dies but is only taken to Avalon by the three Queens for the healing of his most 'grievous wound.' Perhaps during the intervening years he had not only been healed but had made Avalon into a highly fashionable New Age spa, for *something* definitely made it wildly trendy:

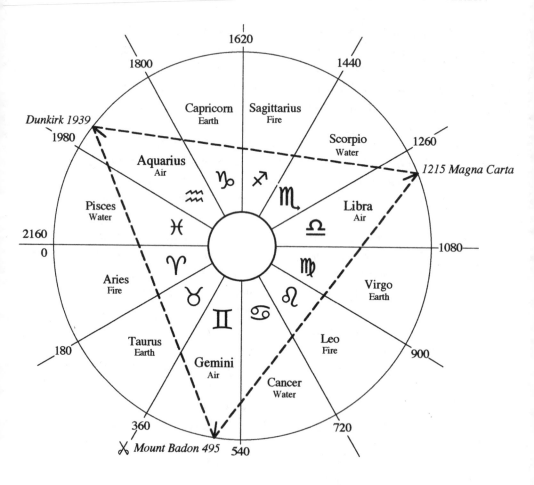

*Fig.31 A grand trine between three victories. There is another grand trine in air
signs between Arthur's great victory over the Saxons at Mount Badon,
the democratic victory of the barons with Magna Carta, and the rise and
defeat of the Counterfeit Grail by Churchill from 1939 to 1945 at Dunkirk
and the Battle of Britain.*

I am going a long way
With these thou seest — if indeed I go —
(For all my mind is clouded with a doubt)
To the island-valley of Avilion;
Where falls not hail, or rain, or any snow,
Nor ever wind blows loudly; but it lies

> Deep-meadow'd, happy, fair with orchard-lawns
> And bowery hollows crown'd with summer sea,
> Where I will heal me of my grievous wound.[29]

Perhaps we can hear an echo of the voice of the healed Arthur in the powerful words of Churchill after Dunkirk:

> In the midst of our defeat, glory came to the Island people, united and unconquerable ... there was a white glow, over-powering, sublime, which ran through our Island from end to end ... and the tale of the Dunkirk beaches will shine in whatever records are preserved of our affairs.[30]

Fig.32 The border country

4. The Other Merlin: Merlin of the Woods

So far we have examined the life of Arthur's Merlin who is usually known as Merlin-Ambrosius or Merlin Emrys on account of his supposed connection with the fifth century British king, Ambrosius Auriolanus, and with the god, Hermes-Mercury. We have assumed that this was the only Merlin that there was, and this would be a reasonable assumption because he is the Merlin about whom almost everyone has heard, and whose deeds always concern King Arthur and the Knights of the Round Table. However, it is not correct to make the assumption that this was the only Merlin that there was, for in 1142 Geoffrey of Monmouth published another book about Merlin, called the *Vita Merlini,* the *Life of Merlin,* which purported to be the sequel to his *The History of the Kings of Britain.*

The scenario of this *Vita Merlini* is very different from that of the earlier *History* and although Geoffrey attempted to weld the two stories together by having the very old Merlin reminisce about the great days of his youth with Arthur, this is unconvincing. For these and various literary reasons, scholars are agreed that to all intents and purposes, Geoffrey has created another Merlin from other source material.

Quite apart from the anachronistic and unconvincing historicity of this composite Merlin, it is clear even to the averagely perceptive reader, that the two Merlins actually have different characters. The Arthurian Merlin, as we have seen, is a magician whose powers to identify the fighting dragons under Vortigern's tower, to build Stonehenge and to effect the conception of Arthur were all very successful and politically important. By comparison, the second, later Merlin of the *Life* is not only unsuccessful, he is a complete political failure. His powers are nothing like as great, are never cast in heroic mould and never rise much above the rather inconsequential gifts of the precognitive seers who are to this day, especially on the Celtic fringes of Britain, still associated with the gift of second sight.

If Arthur's Merlin was called Merlin Emrys or Ambrosius, what is the name of this other Merlin? He is called Merlin the Wild or 'Mad' Merlin because his story is about a prophet King who went out of his mind. He is also called Merlin Silvestris, Merlin of the Woods, because he fled to the woods to find solace and healing. He is also called the Caledonian Merlin because he fled to the wood, or forest of Caledon, which is usually considered to have been in the north of Britain, in what is now Scotland. Yet again he is also called Merlin Lailoken and Merlin Suibhne because two of the sources of his life come from parallel Scottish and Irish traditions associated with the names of these two. Nikolai Tolstoy who, in *The Quest for Merlin,* outlines the complexities of all these, lists the four main sources for this other Merlin:

> Thus four distinct versions of the prophet's career have survived: the *Vita Merlini* of Geoffrey of Monmouth, the Welsh 'Myrddin' poems, the Lailoken episodes, and the story of Suibhne's frenzy. That they all ultimately represent the same saga (though obviously with accretions and distortions acquired along the way) is abundantly clear and is accepted by the best authorities. There also seems little reason to doubt that the nucleus of the Myrddin-Merlin story is substantially historical, and that Myrddin was one of the bards of the sixth century AD whose fame (and, in the cases of Taliesin and Aneirin, their works) has been handed down from earliest times.[31]

It is safe to say that many people do not know that there ever was another Merlin and, because his life is associated with failure not success, that is perhaps understandable. Nevertheless, although it appears to have been a failure we shall find that close inspection *will* yield much of interest and relevance to our theme.

The Vita Merlini

Geoffrey begins his *Vita Merlini* by telling us that Merlin was a famous prophet who was also king of the South Welsh. There came a time of war, civil war between Peredur, prince of the North Welsh and Gwenddolau who ruled the kingdom of Scotland. Merlin joined in and so did Rodarch, king of the Cumbrians. During the battle which followed, two young princes, who were Merlin's close friends, were

Fig.33 The Bard *by Thomas Jones, 1774, shows the dispossessed Welsh bard driven into the wilderness by a hostile army*

killed. Merlin began to mourn them immediately and his lament was heard throughout the army. After the battle he became distraught with grief and although Peredur and the other princes tried to comfort him, he was inconsolable:

> He mourned for his heroes; his flooding tears had no end. He threw dust upon his hair, tore his clothes and lay prostrate on the ground, rolling too and fro ... So for three long days he wept, refusing food, so great the grief that consumed him.[32]

This prolonged anguish began to affect his mind. He began to go mad. This great prophet and king, having suffered the humiliation of defeat and the shock of bereavement, was now becoming deranged. Nothing could be more of a complete contrast to the stories of Arthur's Merlin:

> Then, when the air was full with these repeated loud complainings, a strange madness came upon him. He crept

away and fled to the woods, unwilling that any should see his going. Into the forest he went, glad to lie hidden beneath the ash trees. He watched the wild creatures grazing on the pasture of the glades. Sometimes he would follow them, sometimes pass them in his course. He made use of the roots of plants and of grasses, of fruit from trees and of the blackberries in the thicket. He became a Man of the Woods, as if dedicated to the woods. So for a whole summer he stayed hidden in the woods, discovered by none, forgetful of himself and of his own, lurking like a wild thing.[33]

What could prepare us for this extraordinary development, so early in the story? This is so far from the heroic, mytho-poetic, meta-narrative of Geoffrey's Arthurian *History* that it is difficult to adjust to such a different image. In the *History* we have been examining, and identifying with, the great events in British history which chime with and trine with Arthur's great victory at Mount Badon, for example, Dunkirk and the Battle of Britain. What a shock to discover that hidden within the composite character of Merlin who, in a sense, set all these great Arthurian events in motion, is not a great magician but a blubbering wimp. There is no victory here, not even an honourable defeat because the battle was only a *civil* war which could not even claim to have been a valiant stand against the invading Saxons hordes. This Merlin is a loser. His powers have failed, and he has compounded his defeat by running away to the woods. He, the king of a defeated army, has gone absent without leave. He has shown no officer-like qualities, no stiff upper lip, no British bulldog spirit, no guts. He has proved himself to be a spineless drop-out. This Merlin is no role model. Churchill would have been ashamed of him.

This is all very true if we are determined to judge this second Merlin by the qualities and achievements of the first, Merlin Emrys-Ambrosius. However, if we adjust to the shock of being presented with the story of a *very different* Merlin and accept that he really is a different type of person, then his *Life* becomes fascinating in its own right. If we accept, with the scholars, that Geoffrey pretended that the two Merlins were one and the same and that his ruse has been detected, then let us separate these two Merlins and not expect the second to be like the first.

If we do this, then almost at once, dishonourable though his conduct may have been by strictly military standards, this second Merlin quickly becomes someone who we can get to know. He becomes someone whose experience we can easily recognize and whom we can feel for. Unlike the mytho-poetic, heroic, Arthurian Merlin, he comes close to us because we can see him as an early example of what, today, we call post-traumatic stress disorder. R.J. Stewart in *The Mystic Life of Merlin*, describes this very vividly with regard to American Vietnam and British Great War veterans:

> The flight back to nature and from humanity is a well-known and continuing phenomenon, which develops from the individual stressed beyond endurance in warfare. There are a number of veterans of the Vietnam war in the USA who live to this day in the wilds, as Sylvan men, exactly as described by Geoffrey when telling of Merlin. The shock and horror of their involvement as young men in a horrible dehumanizing war has rendered them unable to be at rest in human society; they return to the heart of nature not in any idealized or pseudo-mystical way, but out of a deep driving necessity to live alone in the woods.
>
> This is not merely a matter of forgetting, but a deep polarization of the soul towards primal life, in an attempt to find the balance destroyed by the evil of war. Such individuals have existed in every land after every war; at one time a number of 'shell-shocked' itinerants from the 1914–1918 Great War could be found in the British countryside, sleeping in the woods, living off the land or from begging. These were not tramps or idle drifters, but men forced to remain outdoors and close to the natural sources of life as a result of the bombardment of the trenches; some of them were entitled to officers' pensions.[34]

It is strange that this is *so* true of this Mad Merlin of the Woods, that we can easily relate to his condition. We can change from condemning him to feeling sorry for him. We can admire Arthur's Merlin, but we can't identify with him. The stories about him are wonderful and awe inspiring but we can't live with them any more than we can live with the heroic moments in our national life. The heroics of war — Dunkirk, the

Battle of Britain, the Blitz, D-Day — are awe-inspiring moments which create heroes. We can live *through* them, if we live at all, but if we live, most of those who survive spend the rest of their lives, as R.J. Stewart rightly says, trying to cope with various levels of post-war traumatic stress. Today, we live in an era where war is no longer thought of as a grand, heroic enterprise. The change in our attitude came during the Great War after years of senseless slaughter in the trenches, when war poets such as Siegfried Sassoon and Wilfred Owen began to tell it the way it was. The pity and horror of war replaced the old admiration for glory and honour. Looked at from the modern disillusionment with war, the madness of Merlin can be seen as a convincing example of what we like to think of as a modern phenomenon, one with which we are deeply sympathetic.

Geoffrey's story goes on to tell us that although Merlin complained a lot about the privations of winter in the wilds, he basically didn't want to go back to court to be with King Rodarch, the Queen Ganieda, who was also his sister, and Guendoloena, his own wife. When Rodarch sent messengers to look for him, he did not want to be found. He preferred to stay in the woods, gradually learning how to adjust himself to the simple austere lifestyle. This raises the theme of the town versus the country, of city life versus the rural idyll, which runs through the rest of the story. This is closely related to that of post-war trauma, but is obviously not the same. It is a theme of many well-known poems down the centuries; to such an extent that it brings Merlin's experience ever closer to our own and all those who are city-bound but who want to 'get away from it all,' to lead the good life, or at least to try and find a rural bolt-hole to which they can escape from another form of madness; the insanity of congested, urban life. This is a typical incident: Merlin was hidden away in the undergrowth and dense hazels of the forest of Caledon. He was overheard talking to an old wolf, complaining about the lack of food which they were both experiencing. A passing traveller, hearing the voice but not seeing anyone, was intrigued and turned aside to investigate.

> He (the traveller) found the place and he found the speaker. But Merlin saw him and was off. The traveller followed, but could not keep up with the fugitive. So he returned to his route and continued on his business; but he was touched by the plight of the man who had fled.[35]

Like most of the incidents in the story, it is graphically told, and comes to life partly because we think we have heard it before. Indeed it is so reminiscent of Matthew Arnold's *Scholar Gipsy* that we might almost assume that this was Arnold's source rather than Glanvil's *Vanity of Dogmatizing* of 1661:

> And near me on the grass lies Glanvil's book
> Come, let me read the oft-read tale again,
> The story of that Oxford scholar poor
> Of pregnant parts and quick inventive brain,
> Who, tir'd of knocking at Preferment's door,
> One summer morn forsook
> His friends, and went to learn the Gipsy lore,
> And roam'd the world with that wild brotherhood,
> And came, as most men deem'd, to little good,
> But came to Oxford and his friends no more.

Some years after his flight to the woods, the Scholar Gipsy met two of his old student friends. He told them that he had learnt much about a different type of knowledge from his Gipsy mates:

> His mates had arts to rule as they desir'd
> The working of men's brains;
> And they can bind them to what thoughts they will:
> 'And I,' he said, 'the secret of their art,
> When fully learn'd, will to the world impart:
> But it needs heaven sent moments for this skill.'

After this the Scholar Gipsy was not encountered again. He was only glimpsed from time to time but if spotted would disappear, just like Merlin. He was 'Seen by rare glimpses,' sitting in the ingle bench of a 'lone alehouse in the Berkshire moors' or at Bab-Lock-Hithe by students returning home late, crossing the ferry or by harvesters bathing in the Thames near Godstow Bridge. They saw him sitting near the river:

> Sitting upon the river bank o'er grown:
> Mark'd thy outlandish garb, thy figure spare,
> Thy dark vague eyes, and soft abstracted air;
> But, when they came from bathing thou wert gone.

Why was Matthew Arnold so moved by the story of the Scholar Gipsy? For the same reason as many romantic poets from Wordsmith to W.B. Yeats. The world was too much with them and they saw little of nature which was theirs. They had to arise and go to their own individual lake isle of Innisfree. Those who found it hardest to escape, felt it the most. Arnold was one of them. He called it 'this strange disease of modern life' and urged the Scholar Gipsy to keep living his life of rural solitude and not to return to 'the infection of our mental strife':

> O born in days when wits were fresh and clear,
> And life ran gaily as the sparkling Thames;
> Before this strange disease of modern life,
> With its sick hurry, its divided aims,
> Its head o'er tax'd, its palsied hearts, was rife —
> Fly hence, our contact fear!
> Still fly, plunge deeper in the bowering wood!
> Averse, as Dido did with gesture stern
> From her false friend's approach in Hades turn,
> Wave us away, and keep thy solitude.[36]

Merlin is eventually prevailed upon by a minstrel, sent by his family to the woods to woo him back. It seemed that the sweet music of the guitar restored his sanity because, unlike the scholar gipsy, he allowed himself to be taken back to the city. On his return he was given a warm welcome. Indeed, the whole court and city turned out to celebrate. This proved too much for him and his madness returned:

> But when Merlin saw such crowds of people there, he could not bear them. He went mad; and once more his derangement filled him with a desire to go off to the forest and he longed to slip away.[37]

Rodarch, the king, then ordered him to be put under guard and tried to persuade him to give up his life in the woods and once again take up his kingship where he 'might wield a royal sceptre and rule a nation of warriors.' But to no avail; even when offered gifts Merlin still preferred the woods. This tussle between his family and his woods is repeated. It is the theme of the first half of the book, but once again he is obsessed with returning to the privations of the forest, even in 'the snow and rain and the angry blast ... Yet that satisfied him more than administering the law in cities and ruling over a warrior people.'

All this seems such a modern problem that it is hard to believe that it existed in the early middle ages. How real was it at that time? Surely Geoffrey couldn't have been speaking about his own experience in the twelfth century, even if it was nevertheless anachronistic to project it back into his imagined recreation of the life of a sixth-century prophet? Or was he? It rather looks as though he could, for historians tell us that the twelfth century saw a phenomenal and unprecedented population explosion and growth in towns: 'Old ones grew, bulging this way and that beyond their ancient walls; new ones were founded both by the king and by private lords.' This growth was linked to technological advances in agriculture. Land clearing, the introduction of crop rotation and the asymmetrical plough, with a mouldboard to turn the soil, all contributed to a tripling of agricultural yield: 'Better tools, collars for draught animals and the use of dung as fertilizer, all help to explain this great advance.' The old Roman *urbs* had changed to the Dark Age fortified *castrum* but now this was changing to something new and dynamic as Alain Erlande-Brandenberg explains in *The Cathedral Builders of the Middle Ages*. For the first time the town-country balance was tipped away from the latter to the former. This began in the eleventh century:

> Towns were born or reborn as a result of the influx of people the country could no longer feed. They were looking for wealth or adventure. A bond was to form between these people of such different backgrounds, that would evolve into a kind of urban patriciate.
>
> Once established, this partnership tended to make the towns both economically and commercially active. The town/country relationship was reversed, with the latter now working for the former.[38]

From these and other accounts of the massive rise in prosperity through agricultural advances, increased trade and communications through better roads and shipping, it can be fairly deduced that Geoffrey was indeed writing about his own times from the point of view of an urban administrator who desperately wanted to get back to nature, having had enough of the stress of ruling a warrior people. More than this, Merlin is representative of those who have psychic gifts and do not want to spend the rest of their lives being caught up in politics and administration. He may be regarded as the prototype of all those who have had to struggle to find their own answer to the competing claims of the artificial, stressful life of the city and the need to get back to the countryside at some point in life.

Although he is tested again and again by his family, Merlin's gift of second sight is used to such good effect, that his brother-in-law, King Rodarch, allows him to return to the woods. Although his sister still tries to stop him, he responds by ordering her to have a house and an observatory built for him in the woods and she agrees. This proves to be the turning point of the story. After this he is allowed to stay in the woods and be served out there by his family and servants. After this he is well on the way to recovering from his madness. His sanity starts returning permanently because he has begun to study the stars seriously. He has become an astrologer and thus taken a stand for another dimension of knowledge which will reveal his true identity and the true destiny of his people. He orders his sister:

> So raise me a house, send me retainers to serve me and pre-
> pare meals in the time when the earth refuses its grain and the
> tree its fruit. Before the other buildings build me a remote one
> to which you will give seventy doors and as many windows,
> through which I may see fire-breathing Phoebus with Venus,
> and watch by night the stars wheeling in the firmament; and
> they will teach me about the future of the nation.
>
> Let there be as many secretaries trained to record what I
> say, and let them concentrate on committing my prophetic
> song to paper. Come here often yourself, dear sister, and
> you will be able to stay my hunger with food and drink.[39]

What Merlin orders is done and thereafter the narrative is full of his prophecies and rather boring sermons about nature. He is back on track. His prophetic gift has been restored.

There is a small but important point which must be made about the number of windows in this observatory. Although the only complete manuscript of Geoffrey's *Life* says there were seventy windows, it is more likely that the supplementary text, quoted by John Matthews in *Taliesin* and in his more recent *King Arthur,* is right when it says that there were seventy-two. The number of windows, because it is for astrological purposes, *has* to be a multiple of twelve and seventy-two allows for six 'windows' in each sign of the zodiac. This in all probability is meant to symbolize and correspond to what is known in astrology as the 'double decanate' system, which allocates each window five degrees or half a decanate. This system as in Figure 34 (see next page), was introduced to the west from the earlier Arab astronomers and would have been part of the repertoire of astrologers such as Adelard of Bath. This variation between seventy and seventy-two in the original texts is replicated in comparable biblical texts, where these two numbers also occur. For instance, in the variant texts which refer to the seventy or seventy-two translators of the Septuagint, the seventy or seventy-two elders who went up Mount Sinai with Moses and the seventy or seventy-two disciples whom Jesus appointed, as well as the twelve apostles, to spread the Gospel round the world. In his book *Taliesin,* John Matthews compares the seventy-two windows with the description of the creation of the universe in the *Saltair ne Rann* and the *Senchus Mor:*

> In the *Vita Merlini,* Merlin studied the heavens from his 'observatory' which had seventy-two windows. In the *Saltair ne Rann* and the *Senchus Mor* this is echoed at the end of the description of the making of the universe, where the passage of the sun through the constellations is described, each of the twelve divisions through which it passes having six windows with close-fitting shutters and strong coverings which open to shed light by day, also making a total of seventy-two.[40]

What is relevant about this from the point of view of this present study, is that this 'double decanate' system corresponds to Charles Carter's zodiac. As can be seen in Figure 34, each zodiac house is divided into six, and each of these divisions is sub-divided into five. Thus $6 \times 5 = 30$. These are the same sub-divisions that are implied by Charles Carter where, with each zodiac sign representing 180 years, each double decanate sub-division represents thirty years ($180 \div 6$) and each degree represents five years. It is strange to think that Merlin might have been using Charles Carter's seventy-two-window zodiac, with the historical value of five years per window, to help him with his prediction of the fortunes of the kings and queens of Britain. It is also intriguing to

Fig.34 A zodiac calendar by Battista Agnese, c. 1550

reflect on what a more detailed examination of European history would
reveal if analysed according to this double-decanate system. However,
such a close inspection must be left to another time.

Merlin's sanity is totally restored much later in the story by the news
that a new spring of pure water has broken out at the foot of the nearby
mountain which proves to be a healing fountain. After Merlin has drunk
fully of it he becomes completely healed. The sudden eruption of this
spring of healing waters is symbolic of Artemis who is the ruler of all
fountains and springs, for in addition to her ancient association with the
Great Bear which was examined in the last chapter, she was also and
more usually connected to the waters of the Goddess and thus with the
waters of the moon.[41]

That this Merlin, this 'mad' Merlin of the Woods, only finds sanity through the healing waters of Artemis is entirely consistent with him as the hermetic figure with whom we have already identified the first Merlin Emrys-Hermes. Now we can see him quite literally as the Hermit which he undoubtedly is. His symbolic animal as a Mercury figure is the wolf who is the *only* animal in the story whom he is recorded as having spoken to, and having shared his early misery with. His whole passion is to lead the life of a wise hermit, not just because urban life, defeat in battle and bereavement have driven him mad but because he is revealing himself as a seeker, a quester, who is following a different calling. He is hearing the voice of nature calling him to get and remain in touch with his primal self; to throw off the mask of kingship and accept a commitment to the power of the Hermetic tradition.

In other accounts of the Arthurian Merlin, as mentioned in the last chapter, we hear of him having Excalibur, Arthur's famous sword, fashioned in the workshops of the Lady of the Lake, deep under her dark waters. Excalibur symbolizes the sovereignty of the land which is given to the king by the goddess. Artemis is that Goddess. She is goddess of the waters of the land and of the waters of the moon. This story of Merlin being healed by drinking the miraculous waters of the newly discovered fountain is similar in symbolic importance to that of Excalibur. It tells us that he has at last discovered the link between the sovereignty of the land and the stars. In the cycle of the epochs of the Age of Pisces, as defined by Charles Carter, by the time these stories actually happened, in so far as they were historical, the epoch of Gemini had ended and the epoch of Cancer had begun. So the rulership of Mercury had given way to that of the Moon. Cancer is ruled by the Moon goddess, by the very waters that healed mad Merlin. The time of Artemis had come. Is that why his story is so very different from that of Arthur's Merlin? His character reflects the qualities of Cancer, the cardinal water sign. He had to develop from merely reflecting the mercurial qualities of Gemini, his own mutable air home-sign. This was a great change. He had to fail in the one to achieve new success in the other. He had to break down before he could break through to it. He had to go mad in order to achieve a new sanity and learn his 'Gipsy lore;' be a lunatic until he came to understand the power of the Cancerian moon's wisdom. Above all, he had to recognize that what he learnt about the moon was manifested in the healing waters of the underground stream that welled up miraculously. As above so below. He was still Mercury the hermit but he was now most definitely and more completely also the servant of the goddess.

Merlin of the Woods — the historical context

As mentioned before, Nikolai Tolstoy tells us that 'the nucleus of the Myrddin-Merlin story is substantially historical.' Merlin, he says, was one of the sixth century bards, along with Taliesin and Aneirin whose poetry and stories, albeit in later format, have come down to us. King Rodarch, Merlin's brother-in-law, can be identified. He is Rhydderch, King of Strathclyde. Guennolous, against whom the fateful battle was fought, was prince Gwenddolau of the Gododdin. Likewise Ganieda is Gwenddydd, Rhydderch's queen and Telgelinus, who visits the mad Merlin and ends up deciding to stay in the woods with him because he had 'spent long enough in empty living,' is his fellow bard Taliesin.

The fateful battle itself has been identified as the Battle of Arderydd fought in 575, between Longtown and Carwinley, north-east of Carlisle. Research into the multiple sources of this northern tradition, especially those regarding the figure of Lailoken, has revealed considerable detail about this battle, as Geoffrey Ashe explains:

> However, the Welsh give more details of the battle. It was recalled and mourned by the bards as 'futile,' having been fought over a lark's nest. The phrase is a bitter joke, referring to Caerlaverock, the Fort of the Lark, a stronghold on the north side of the Solway Firth which was evidently a theme of contention. The battle took place in Arderydd, now the parish of Arthuret, in Cumbria near the Border. One of the chief leaders was Gwenddolau, and the precise location was close to his own stronghold, Caer Gwenddolau, another name that was corrupted and is now Carwinley. Myrddin, as the Welsh called him, fought on Gwenddolau's side. Their enemies were other Britons, some of them kinsmen, so that the battle had the special horror of civil war. The most important was King Rhydderch of Strathclyde, who appears also in the Lailoken matter. In the Welsh accounts, it is not so clear that Myrddin was actually to blame for the battle. But the slaughter was fearful, and his partial guilt caused him to be shunned and drove him into his forest wanderings half out of his mind, with sequels related in the stories calling him Lailoken.[42]

Fig.35 Remains of a fort at Liddel, near Longtown, where the Battle of Arderydd is believed to have taken place

Fig.36 Merlin sites along the River Tweed

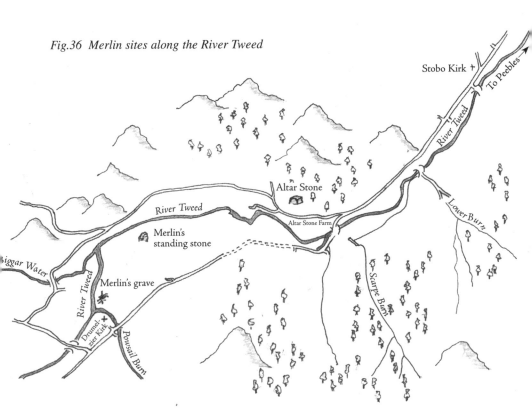

Fig.37 The church at Arderydd, the old name for Longtown, Cumbria

Other stories in the Merlin-Lailoken material link his name with his
contemporary St Kentigern. He is said to have interrupted the saint's
sermons near Hoddom, Dumfriesshire, with wild inarticulate prophecies. He is also said to have presented himself for baptism at the Saint's
church at Stobo and to have suffered a threefold death at Drumelzier at
the hands of retainers of the local prince Meldred, the next day. The date
of his death is unknown but, if there is any truth in these stories, must
have been before 612 when Kentigern died.

The Battle of Arderydd took place in 575 and Merlin must have
died sometime before 612, so we can say that all the stories of his life,
whether as Geoffrey's Merlin of the Woods, or as Lailoken or Suibhne,
may be considered to have taken place between these two dates. If we
place these dates on Charles Carter's epoch of Cancer, which started in
540, we get 5.8° for 575 (575 − 540 = 35 ÷ 6 = 5.8) and 12° for 612 (612
− 540 = 72 ÷ 6 = 12).

Contrary to received opinion over the centuries, the events relating
to the life of Merlin Silvestris-Lailoken-Suibhne, took place in what is
today called Southern Scotland, *not* Wales or England and which in the
sixth century was known as 'the North,' *y gogledd*. This is very intriguing because just as we have discovered that the characters of the two

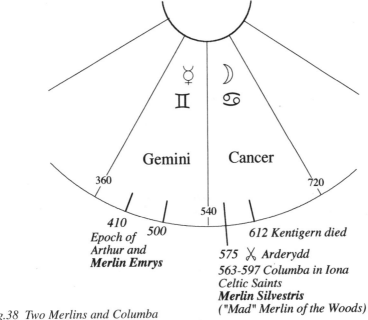

Fig.38 Two Merlins and Columba

Merlins are very different from one another, now we find that so is the geographical area of their activity. While both were obviously British and it would be anachronistic to call them anything else, yet as history later developed, it could be said that Arthur's Merlin was Welsh-British while mad Merlin of the Woods was Scottish-British. Since we have now discovered that the people and the places associated with the story of his madness have been identified historically, it would be of great interest to see if his urge to move from a political and military life to that of a hermit, was unique for that period, or whether it can be seen as representative of a contemporary trend. Geoffrey of Monmouth portrays his second Merlin as a unique, almost pathological case, but how unique or odd was he for his time? Now that we know his dates, let us see whether there were others with whom we might be able to compare him.

The striking thing which can immediately be said about this period in the north of Britain is that it coincides almost exactly with what is called the great age of the Celtic saints. The greatest of these was St Columba who, like Merlin, had been a prince and who, like Merlin, had been disgraced because of stirring up a disastrous civil war and had renounced his political and military life in favour of that of an austere monk leading a simple, ascetic life. This comparison, however strange it may seem to those more familiar with the outline of Columba's life than with that of Geoffrey's *Vita Merlini,* is nevertheless most marked. It is also extraordinary that Columba was only one generation older than his 'fictional' contemporary, for he was born in 521 while Merlin, who was obviously still young at the time of the battle in 575, was probably born in the 540s. Although Columba came to Scotland in 563, he probably did not settle on Iona until the early 570s, about the time of the Battle of Arderydd. He died in 597 while Merlin probably lived on into the early seventh century.

Yet again a comparison can be made between Merlin's continuous close family relationship with the political world, despite his passion for the hermit's life, and that of Columba, and his ecclesiastical peers. For they too were closely related to the courts of kings and like their Druid forebears were often counsellors to princes as well as ascetic hermits. There is even a comparison with regard to magic which, as Michael Lynch points out in *Scotland, a New History,* it was obligatory to display in order to prove one's holiness:

> The first duties of holy men were as the magicians and clerks of kings rather than acting as their conscience. Magic was demonstrated at the inauguration of a king or at his victory in battle; Aedan mac Gabrain prospered after he was ordained by Columba as King of Dalriada in 574 but his grandson Domnall Brecc met with a series of catastrophes ending in his death in 642 because, it was said, he had breached the promise made by his own kindred to remain faithful to Iona and the Irish family of Cenel Conaill ...The literate clergy were a mandarin class which forged a role for itself as the advocates and interpreters of high kingship. Columba and Adamnan concerned themselves with overkings, of Dalriada and of Picts, who were worthy of Christian record, like kings of Judah and Israel.[43]

Even the way in which Adamnan's *Life of Columba* portrayed Iona as a 'small and remote island of the Britannic ocean' conjures up an image similar to the remote woods of Merlin, while his portrayal of Columba himself as a simple holy monk, is almost indistinguishable from the characteristics which Geoffrey's Merlin displays. Indeed, there are so many positive comparisons, that it could almost be said that in the company of a random selection of Columba's holy men, Merlin would

Fig.39 Columba, Scottish National Portrait Gallery

probably have passed unnoticed. Even his Christian credentials would have passed muster because Geoffrey records that he prayed and gave thanks to God as king and creator and on more than one occasion called on Christ to help him in his early travails: 'Oh Christ, God of heaven, what shall I do? What place is there on earth where I can live.'

For all these reasons it is possible to maintain that Geoffrey's *Vita Merlini* tells the story of a life which may still in certain details be called unique but which, to a large extent, is indistinguishable from the lives of many holy men of that period. These were men who led real recorded lives and left a lasting legacy of missionary work all over Scotland; men like Comgall of Bangor and Brendan of Clonfert who founded monasteries on Tiree and the Garvellach Islands. Or Moluag, Donnan and Maelrubai who did the same on Lismore, Eigg and round Wester Ross. But they were also men who spread the influence of the Celtic, Columban church much further afield, to England and the continent of Europe. For instance, Aidan, a Columban monk from Iona established a monastery on Lindisfarne in

634. Others took it to Burgundy, to St Gall in Switzerland and Bobbio in the Apennines. Many Irish and Ionian monks also travelled to what is now central and southern Germany and founded Columban houses such as Kilian in Würzburg and Virgil in Salzburg.

It would seem as though, despite being written in the mid-twelfth century, Geoffrey had discovered new source material and was so faithful to it, that his second Merlin truly displayed characteristics which were typical of the actual age of these sources. He had succeeded in portraying a Merlin who, contrary to our conventional image of him, was in fact representative of the spirit of the period in which he was said to have lived, that is, the sixth, not the fifth, century. This period is famous in history as the golden age of the Celtic saints, among whom, odd though it may seem, we can appropriately place him.

The Other Merlin trine

Having placed our Other Merlin right in the middle of the Great Age of the Celtic saints, let us see whether we can find an obvious and important trine to which we can easily relate him, or at least what we feel he represented. It would be good to know whether the grand trine in Air signs, which we identified successfully in the last chapter, could be replicated. Can the Zodiac of the Grail be prevailed upon to yield further secrets through Water signs?

We move through the epochs of Cancer, Leo, Virgo and Libra and arrive at the period in Scorpio between 1295 and 1320 (that is, 575, the Battle of Arderydd plus 720 and 600 plus 720). The epoch of Scorpio, the fixed water sign ruled by Mars and Pluto, was characterized by Charles Carter by certain nasty phenomena such as massacres, torture, the Black Death and the Hundred Years War. It was also defined by him as the time of 'endless Anglo-Scottish conflicts' and, on a higher level, with an 'age of Christian mysticism; one finds such names as Tauler, Ruysbroek, Julian of Norwich.' This is intriguing because according to most historians, at least with Scottish sympathies, this period is called the great age of the Scottish Wars of Independence, while according to Matthew Fox, in his influential book *Original Blessing,* the Creation Spirituality of which he is the chief modern spokesman, can be traced back to the Columban age in the sixth century via the age of the Rhineland mystics in the thirteenth and fourteenth centuries. He says that the latter were derived from and

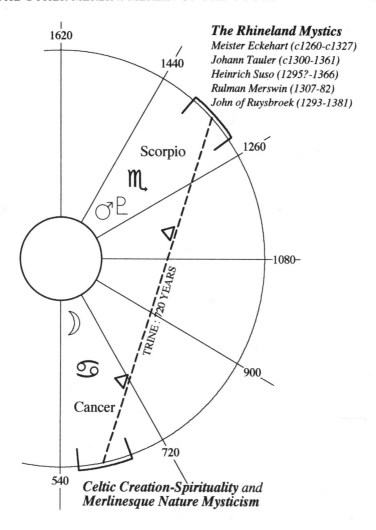

Fig.40 Merlin's nature mysticism and the trine with the Rhineland mystics

the heirs of the former. In all his writings he, unconsciously, proclaims a harmonious trine relationship between the two:

> Yet it was the Celts who settled along the Rhine and deep into Germany and Northern Italy and who laid the spiritual groundwork for the great creation-centred Rhineland mystics including Hildegarde, Mechtild, Eckhart and even Francis of Assisi.[44]

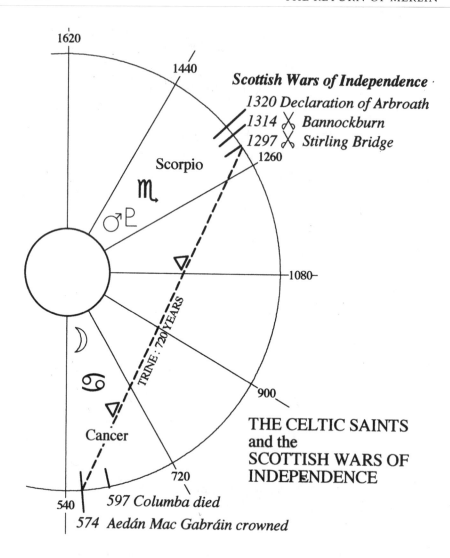

Fig.41 Columban missions and 'king making'

With regard to the Scottish Wars of Independence, it is immediately apparent that there is also an easily recognizable trine relationship between the great days of William Wallace and Robert the Bruce, on the one hand, and the era of the Celtic saints on the other. This is exemplified by Wallace's victory at Stirling Bridge in 1297 which trine's almost exactly with Columba's crowning or ordination of Aedan mac Gabrain as King of Dalriada, in 574. It is also in an almost exact trine with the fateful Battle of Arderydd after which Merlin went mad but which, in the long term, seems to have worked as much for the growing success of the Kingdom of Strathclyde as it did for the long term spiritual transformation of Merlin. It is also exemplified in Robert the Bruce's great victory at Bannockburn in 1314, which trines exactly with 594 and Columba's last years. It would seem as though the Cancerian energies embodied in the spiritual and political acumen of the great Columba had somehow been transferred across the centuries to those in the equivalent degree of Scorpio. Or was it something more profound to do with the land? It was suggested previously that Merlin of the Woods had eventually connected with the goddess of the land. Her healing spring had suddenly sprung up miraculously and he had been finally cured of his madness. This was Artemis. Her hour had come for she was goddess of the moon and the moon is the ruler of the epoch of Cancer. Was there some profound link between her lunar energies and those of Mars and Pluto, the two rulers of Scorpio?

Fig.42 Robert the Bruce and William Wallace, Scottish National Portrait Gallery

Were they connected mainly because Cancer and Scorpio are both water signs and water signs are somehow involved with the destiny of Scotland? This connection between Cancer and Scotland would certainly agree with the judgment of William Lilly, the famous seventeenth-century astrologer, in his book, *Christian Astrology*.[45] Whatever the reason, it seems that we have moved along a trine of 720 years from one great period in Scottish history to another. This is equally true of the Declaration of Arbroath in 1320.

The Declaration of Arbroath is arguably the most important document in Scottish history. In its simple appeal to the right of Scottish sovereignty and its definition of the right relationship between King and people, it is equivalent to Magna Carta and, to this day, has the status of a surrogate Scottish constitution. Michael Lynch explains its timeless appeal:

> The simplicity of its language has much to do with the Declartion's timeless appeal: in the course of little more than 1,200 words it managed to condense a mythology of the nation's past, provide a compelling vision of the relationship of the King of Scots and the Scottish people, and summarize the history of the present struggle as one in which the issue was 'for liberty alone that we fight and contend for, which no honest man will lose but with his life.'[46]

Is it only a coincidence that if we go back 720 years to circa 600 Columba had just died, but his spiritual war band, the monks of his church militant, were winning more spiritual victories across Scotland and Europe, than at any other time? Is it pure coincidence that their message of creation-spirituality, that God has two books — the Bible and the book of his Creation — was at that time laying the foundation for a spiritual tradition of inclusivity in church and state, of one Cancerian family under God which, like the underground stream that healed Merlin, appeared once again 720 years later? I think not. There are too many coincidences here. There is a pattern emerging; a pattern of inclusivity, with easily recognizable connections between culture and Christ, Merlin and Columba; where the boundaries between their differences are to some extent blurred; where, the All is connected to the One, and the One to the All. This strange similarity between the life of Columba and that of Merlin, which Nikolai Tolstoy also notes between St Kentigern and Merlin, seems to be replicated in the Platonic realism of one of the most famous mystics of the late thirteenth and early fourteenth century, Meister Eckhart (1260–1327). As an exact contemporary of the resurgence of the Scottish fortunes and as a representative of the tradition of this Creation Spirituality which had been brought to Germany by the Celtic saints seven hundred years before, he speaks eloquently of this inclusivity. Williston Walker in *A History of the Christian Church,* summarizes his seminal contribution and the trouble into which it got him:

> An important representative of this mystical spirit was 'Meister' Eckhart (1260–1327), a German Dominican, who studied in Paris, served as provincial prior of the Saxon district, lived for a time in Strasburg, and taught in Cologne. At the close of his life Eckhart was under trial for heresy. He himself declared his readiness to submit his opinions to the judgment of the church, but two years after his death a number of his teachings were condemned by Pope John XXII. In true Neo-Platonic fashion Eckhart taught that that which is real in all things is the divine. In the soul of man is a spark of God. That is the true reality in all men. All individualizing qualities are essentially negative. Man should therefore lay them aside. His struggle is to have God born in his soul, that is to enter into full communion with and to come under the control of the in-dwelling God. In this effort Christ is the pattern and example in whom Godhead dwelt in humanity in all fullness. With God dominant, the soul is filled with love and righteousness. Churchly observances may be of some value, but the springs of the mystic life are far deeper and its union with God more direct. Good works do not make righteous. It is the soul already righteous that does good works. The all-important matter is that the soul enters into its full privilege of union with God.[47]

Eckhart had a huge influence. His chief followers were John Tauler (d. 1361), Henry Suso (d. 1366), Rulman Merswin (1307–82) and John of Ruysbroeck (1294–1381), who in turn had a great influence on the early Reformers. Martin Luther found them 'evangelical' and claimed that Eckhart was a Protestant before Protestantism. Who would have thought that the tradition which began over 700 years before and which we have identified as being supremely identified with Columba *and* Merlin of the Woods, should have had such a long run! Who would have thought that these two periods of historical importance would have been in a trine relationship!

The other Merlin Grand trine

Now that we have established a trine relationship between 575 and 600 in the epoch of Cancer and 1295 and 1320 in Scorpio, we must go on to discover whether this trine can be progressed another 720 years into the mutable water sign of Pisces. What dates do we come to? Adding 720 to 1295 gives us the year 2015 and adding 720 to 1320 gives us 2040. Here we hit a problem because both 2015 and 2040 are well into the future. What can we do about this? Could we assume that we are at the beginning of another great era in Scotland's history? Would it be presumptuous to assume that because the trine between the early degrees of Cancer and those of Scorpio has been convincing, that there will be another trine the beginnings of which we can already discern?

Let's be presumptuous and make this assumption. To make it an exercise which may bring this nearer to us, let us regress the trines by nine years from 1295 to 1286. This was the fateful year which saw the tragic, accidental death of Alexander III which precipitated the dynastic struggle, which led to the attempts of Edward I to reduce Scotland to a feudal fiefdom. Many have noticed that there is something in the Scottish psyche which needs to experience defeat in order to trigger off victory. It is a more extreme example of the Dunkirk spirit. After all, the Battle of Arderydd was a disaster. Likewise the Battle of Catterick Bridge of circa 600, which sparked off the Scottish equivalent of the Arthurian resistance. Even the victories of Wallace and Bruce were qualified because, if seen as battles for Independence, then that Independence was only relative. If we adopt Duke Senior's paradox: 'Sweet are the uses of adversity; which like the toad, ugly and venomous, Wears yet a precious jewel in his head,' as our motto, then a much more positive prospect looms before us. So, if we bring

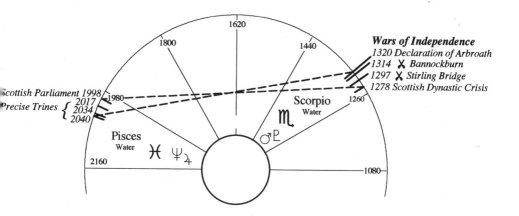

Fig.43 Precise trines with the Wars of Independence. Do these herald a period of coming greatness for the North?

the trine from 1286 up to 2006 it is easier to draw a parallel with the present developments. By this I mean the developments in political devolution.

Take, for example, the film *Braveheart,* which was released in 1997 to celebrate the seven hundredth anniversary of Wallace's victory at Stirling Bridge, and created a huge wave of positive feeling for Scotland's most heroic era. It also coincided with the setting up of the Scottish Parliament after nearly three hundred years in the following year. Is it only a coincidence that 1997 was called the Year of the Celtic saints because it was exactly 1400 years after the death of St Columba? Remembering that in the computation of our trines, we are allowed an 'orb' or 2° degrees of latitude — that is, twelve years, 1400 years — while not precise, may be taken as a very close approximation.

That said, we may still distinguish between seven hundred years as an approximate trine and 720 which is a precise one. Therefore, we may legitimately expect that when the precise trine comes in 2017 we will experience a much more powerful vibration. Likewise, when we celebrate Bannockburn's seven hundredth anniversary in 2014 we will still have twenty years to go before the exact trine in 2034.

This will also be the case when we commemorate the seven hundredth anniversary of the Declaration of Arbroath in 2020. The exact trine vibration will not hit us until 2040. In other words, if there is any 'truth' in this

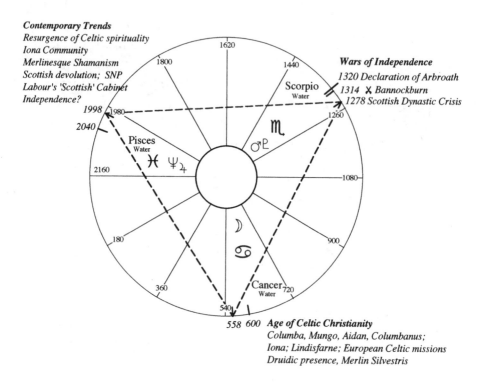

Contemporary Trends
Resurgence of Celtic spirituality
Iona Community
Merlinesque Shamanism
Scottish devolution; SNP
Labour's 'Scottish' Cabinet
Independence?

Wars of Independence
1320 Declaration of Arbroath
1314 ✗ Bannockburn
1278 Scottish Dynastic Crisis

Age of Celtic Christianity
Columba, Mungo, Aidan, Columbanus;
Iona; Lindisfarne; European Celtic missions
Druidic presence, Merlin Silvestris

Fig.44 Scotland's grand trine

Other Merlin's Scottish trine, then it should be possible to predict a period
of coming greatness for Scotland. This may be doubly 'true' for according
to Charles Carter's system we will still be in the Age of Pisces as well as
in the epoch of Pisces for another 150 years, and so the Neptunian energies
of this mutable water sign, should be very strong indeed.

From this study of the two Merlins, Merlin Emrys-Ambrosius and
Merlin of the Woods, there have emerged two grand trines, one in air
signs and one in water signs, which seem to be closely connected to significant periods in the history of England and of Scotland. It is strange
that in some mysterious way, if taken together, they have helped us to
identify some events and characteristics, which could be associated
uniquely with Britain as a whole. The ancient notion of 'the Matter of
Britain' seems to be more than a mytho-poetic concept. It seems to have
been working away over the centuries in the actual historical development of England and Scotland together. Could it be that Britain is still,

as it was first known to be, 'Merlin's Precinct'? And can Merlin still be identified as an embodiment of that Mercury who Caesar said was anciently our chief God? It looks as if this may well be so. If our discoveries about the Zodiac of the Grail and our initial successes in uncovering two of its grand trines are anything to go by, then, who knows where other revelations will lead us? A period of coming greatness can be predicted for Scotland as the energies of the epoch of Pisces-Pisces continue to become more powerful. We can't say exactly what will happen, but we know it will be a great adventure. With Merlin as our magus, we know it will be momentous, perhaps another golden age.

5. The Renaissance of Wonder

In the *The Da Vinci Code* Leigh Teabing suggests to Sophie that the motive for Opus Dei murdering the leaders of the Priory of Sion is that it is a preemptive strike because they fear that the Priory will reveal the secrets of the Holy Blood Line. When Sophie asks why that should happen *now* when the secrets had been kept hidden for centuries, he said that Opus Dei might have become jumpy because the turn of the millennium signalled the end of the Age of Pisces and the start of the Age of Aquarius. The Age of Pisces was characterized by people being told what to think about spiritual truth whereas the Age of Aquarius encourages people to think for themselves. So they struck before the devastating news leaked out anyway and destroyed the credibility of the church.

This is a most ingenious use of the Age change as the crucial factor in the drama and, as far as it goes, contains enough astrological truth to carry conviction. Not many astrologers would deny that the Piscean ideal, among other things, 'believes that man must be told what to do by higher powers' ... Or that 'Now, however, we are entering the Age of Aquarius — the water bearer whose ideals claim that man will learn the truth and be able to think for himself.'[48]

The problem about this thesis is not that it isn't a tenable astrological interpretation, or that it doesn't work well in the drama because it works very effectively. The problem is that while it is tenable as far as it goes, it is only one among many theories about when the Age of Pisces ends and Aquarius begins. There are so many theories that Nicholas Campion, who has listed about seventy of them, declares that they vary so much that their lack of precision renders them of little astrological value.[49] However, debateable point though this is, we are committed in this study to the particular theory of Charles Carter, who believed that the Age of Pisces began with the birth of Christ and will only end in the year 2160. This is called the 'Equal House' theory because it is based on the division of the Great Year of 25 920 years into twelve equal houses or Ages, which comes out at 2 160 years each.

So, the weakness with Dan Brown's use of the theory that the Age of Pisces ended around the year 2000, is not that it isn't a real option, but that it differs radically from Charles Carter and his theory that the Age

can be divided into twelve houses or epochs of 180 years. If the Age
of Aquarius has begun already, then there has been no time nor space
for the epoch of Pisces. This of course is of no consequence to Dan
Brown, but it is to us because it is only by the inclusion of the twelfth
house epoch — that is, Pisces — that I believe we can do justice to
the forces of Neptune, or understand the pervasive Neptunian *timbre*
of our times.

Charles Carter's system depends on there being an epoch of Pisces.
Talk about the New Age is usually astrologically simplistic and, the
process of moving towards the New Age is so slow that little beyond
generalizations can be said about it. This general movement of the
Ages tells us very little about the movement of Carter's epochs from
Aquarius to Pisces. Once we acknowledge that this is indeed what
is happening then the first thing which must be understood is that
although the two processes are going in opposite directions both,
nevertheless, involve the relationship between Pisces and Aquarius.
The Ages are moving from Pisces to Aquarius while the epochs are
moving from Aquarius to Pisces. In other words, according to this
theory, whichever way we look at it, we are living at a time which is
saturated by the old rulers of Pisces and Aquarius, namely Jupiter and
Saturn, as well as the new rulers, Neptune and Uranus. Consequently,
the general pervasiveness of these Neptunian and Uranian energies,
resulting from the effect of the 1993 Neptune-Uranus conjunction, is
lasting much longer than it should have done, had it not been boosted
by Jupiter and Saturn's compatible energies. Many of the other features, which Tarnas lists as the consequences of this conjunction,
are still with us and are still increasing. Astrologer Dawne Kovan
points out that, in addition, this conjunction occurred three times in
1993–94, and within half a degree of a fourth, thus greatly increasing
its potency. For example:

> We see this all around us now: the tremendous upswelling of
> interest today in an astonishing multiplicity of spiritual paths
> and traditions, in esoteric disciplines, in the transpersonal
> movement, in meditation and mystical religious traditions,
> in Jungian and archetypal psychology, in mythology and
> ancient religions, in shamanism and indigenous traditions,
> in the recovery of Goddess spirituality and feminine dimen-
> sions of the divine, in ecofeminist spirituality, in psychedelic

self-exploration and new forms of experiential psycho-
therapy that effect profound changes of consciousness, in
the emergence of holistic and participatory paradigms in
virtually every field, in the unprecedented convergence of
science and spirituality.[50]

It has been proposed that the discovery of Neptune in 1848 gave an
extra boost to the Neptune-Uranus conjunction of 1821, and that the
discovery of Uranus and the coming of the epoch of Aquarius both
enhanced the Uranian part of this conjunction. Now, the same interpretation is being adopted to explain why the Neptunian part of the 1993 conjunction remains so powerful. Coupled with the continuous movement
towards the Age of Aquarius, it would amount to an ambience somewhat
similar to a continuous Neptune-Uranus conjunction. The continuation
of the effects of the 1993 conjunction are indicated as much in the positive ways, such as those listed by Tarnas, as in the negative ways, which
he also enumerates:

The collective psyche's highly activated thirst for transcend-
ence, while ultimately spiritual in nature, has brought forth
a wide range of less exalted impulses and behaviour. The
collective impulse towards escapism and denial, passivity
and narcissism, credulity and delusion; the hyper-stimulat-
ing rapidity of technologically produced images signify-
ing nothing; the hypnotic fascination with and addiction
to image ('image is everything'); indeed, the widespread
obsession with addictions of all kinds, from drugs and
alcohol to consumerism and television ... (We see sug-
gestive signs of a disruptively hyperactivated Neptune on
more literal levels as well, with massive floods, tidal waves,
disasters at sea, oil spills, industrial accidents involving
liquids and gases.) The intensified religious consciousness
of the age has given rise to cult movements, fundamentalist
fanaticism and a host of eccentric 'new age ' infatuations.
The dissolving of rigid structures in the psyche permitting
the emergence of non-ordinary states of consciousness can
lend itself not only to higher levels of consciousness and
genuine mystical illumination, but to destructively delusory
states as well.[51]

This is equally the case if we look at the old rulers of Pisces and Aquarius, namely Jupiter and Saturn. The twenty-year conjunctions of these two great planets have been definitive of much of the development of western history, according to traditional astrologers. This is not the time to amplify this except to say that astrologers attribute the phenomenal growth of secular materialism during the last 150 years to the Saturn-Jupiter conjunction of 1842, which was in Capricorn, and that the cycle of these conjunctions is still under this dominating influence and will be for another fifty years.

However, there is a positive side to this same consumerism and commercialization. It is said to have also led to the development of the festival of Christmas, albeit closely bound-up with this secular materialism, as an extraordinarily powerful time of joviality, generosity and concern for children and the elderly. One of Jupiter's most positive qualities is joviality. Indeed his Latin name was Jove and one of Saturn's major qualities is age and the aging process. The figure of Santa Claus, or Father Christmas, is the personification of these; he is the epitome of joviality and age, the jolly old man. This personification takes place because every year these two separate energies meet at mid-winter, for the month up to December 21 is Sagittarius, which is ruled by jovial Jupiter and from December 21 Capricorn takes over, ruled by old Saturn. After twelve days of joining forces for a special joint initiative — recognized in ancient Celtic lands as Yule Tide and in Roman culture as the Saturnalia — they cease to be conjunct and go their separate ways. The decorations are taken down, Saturn changes his role into that of the Grim Reaper and the obituary columns fill up with his harvesting work. The mythology of Christmas is all astral, and who today would deny that Santa comes from the stars, some say the North Pole, or that his reindeer, although from Lapland, have special astral stables? This is very much as it should be for the star, which we are told was followed by the astrologers, the erstwhile wise men, was none other than a triple conjunction of Jupiter and Saturn. It led them to the first Christmas at Bethlehem and it still leads us to ours.

These illustrations are the most obvious contemporary examples of how astral forces can come together in such a powerful way that they become personified in a complex living mythology. This is the essence of the ancient hermetic tradition with its fabulous axiom of the Emerald Tablet: 'As above, so below,' as in the stars, so on the earth. This was what we claimed for the personification of Merlin and Arthur. They came

'alive' through the writings of Geoffrey of Monmouth, as the personification of the astral forces of the 1136 Neptune-Uranus conjunction in
Libra, for this conjunction was itself conjunct with Arcturus — Arthur's
star, which was also at 12° Libra. This is the theme of this study and it
would seem that it has been the Neptune-Uranus conjunction cycle of
171 years, that has given us the fixed points from which we have been
able to assess Charles Carter's theory of epochs.

From the analysis of the double movement of the close relationship
between the two *new* rulers of the Ages, namely Neptune and Uranus
on the one hand, and the two new rulers of the epochs, namely Uranus
and Neptune on the other, we can deduce that their combination is producing a Uranus-Neptune, Neptune-Uranus 'double whammy.' Their
effect, which has already been incalculable, can be predicted to continue
to increase. One thing at least is certain, that the 'birth' of many more
Arthurian and Merlinesque figures can be expected. In Glastonbury
alone, according to a recent Warden of Chalice Well, people believing
themselves to be Arthur, Guinevere or Merlin appear there annually
— on average, three Arthurs, two Merlins and one Guinevere each year.
This should not be surprising when we remember that Glastonbury itself
could be said to have had its 'new birth' in the 1890s, around the time
of the Neptune-Pluto conjunction of 1891. Also the psychic experiences of Dr John Goodchild and Wellesley Tudor-Pole, by which the
Chalice was first discovered in Italy and then taken to and rediscovered
in Glastonbury, set the scene for the re-emergence of all these latter day
Arthurian characters.

I believe that the three influences of (1) the Age Change from Pisces
to Aquarius; (2) the epoch change from Aquarius to Pisces, and (3) the
sustained influence of the Neptune-Uranus conjunction of 1993 have
combined to create a climate of Neptunian fantasy, which makes it
increasingly difficult to distinguish between fact and fiction, myth and
the personification of myth. The phenomenal success of *The Da Vinci
Code* is a supreme example of this. Likewise, *The Holy Blood and the
Holy Grail.* In both, the thesis, which they exploit, is the assumption that
Jesus was married and had a family. Yet this is but an extreme example
of the need to restore the fortunes of the feminine and the goddess. The
growth of the feminist movement has been with us for many years now,
and was strong in the 1980s at the start of the epoch of Pisces, when the
forces of Neptune began to take over from Uranus. Pisces, the fishes,

is a feminine sign and Neptune is a feminine energy. The repression of the feminine during most of the Age of Pisces has been a travesty of the true nature of Pisces and of Neptune. The subjection and destruction of the ecosphere is the outward expression of this repression. This has been said for many years by eco-feminists. What has also been said is that this is the time for 'the return of the repressed,' to use a Jungian concept, which can also be attributed, like most of Jung's work, to the effects of the same Neptune-Pluto conjunction of 1891. The 'Return of the Repressed,' or the manifestation of the true nature of Pisces and of Neptune, carries with it the Plutonic process of clearing away the accretions of patriarchy from over the centuries. It is not surprising that this should appear, be almost personified, in the 'belief' that Jesus was married and had a family. Dan Brown and the authors of *The Holy Blood and the Holy Grail* (published significantly in 1982) have produced a reinterpretation of the origins and development of the Christian Church, which is consonant with these newly enhanced Piscean and Neptunian energies. Neptune is said to rule the arts. All art is illusion but also all great art uses illusion to mediate 'truth.' Such is the paradox with which Neptune presents us, particularly with regard to *The Holy Blood and the Holy Grail* and *The Da Vinci Code*. During the next one hundred years the flood of alternative histories and fictional-fantasies may so grip the collective imagination that to all intents and purposes the speculation about Jesus' family may become an article of 'faith,' and replace the Virgin Birth as a myth for our time. The latter can already be seen as a convenient myth, or even a con, for the influence of the zodiac sign Virgo, complementary to Pisces, interpreted as a nit-picking spinster, itself a caricature of Virgo.

Astrology itself is likewise experiencing a 'return of the repressed' in the collective psyche. This is doing, and will continue to do, much to restore the feminine and indeed the goddess, because astrology has always represented the study of the balance of opposites through the balance of its six masculine and six feminine houses. It is significant that when the resurgence of medieval astrology in the epoch of Scorpio (a feminine sign) was replaced by Sagittarius (a masculine sign), the collective psyche moved towards first the rejection of astrology and then the persecution of witches, via the reformation and the counter-reformation.

These days it is different because we have moved on from the epoch of Aquarius which is masculine to that of Pisces which is feminine, and it is thus not surprising that the balance of opposites has become a regulative concept in our time, particularly through the influence of Eastern philosophers, who have had a less traditional masculine bias. The mythological symbol of the yin/yang dragons round the *axis mundi* was the Caduceus of Mercury as explained in Chapter 2. Mercury was Hermes and Merlin was an alias for the Mercury-Hermes tradition, which came back into Britain via such twelfth-century scholars as Adelard of Bath. This was the basis of our Hermetic interpretation of the story of Merlin's discovery of the two dragons fighting under Vortigern's tower. They represented the two forces of the earth in relation to the powers of the cosmos, being energized sufficiently to shake off the claims of the usurping invaders in favour of the indigenous people who had stayed in tune with the ancient energies of the land.

This theme of the balance of opposites has re-emerged on a massive scale in our time which may be another reason why the story of Merlin, Vortigern and the fighting dragons has once more assumed such importance. Richard Tarnas itemizes this theme in more general, cosmic terms:

> We see it (the effects of the Neptune-Uranus conjunction) in the collective awakening of an intense desire to merge with a greater unity — to reconnect with the Earth and all forms of life on it, with the cosmos, with the community of being. We see it in the powerful new awareness of *anima mundi,* the soul of the world. And we see it in the widespread urge to overcome old separations and dualisms — between human beings and nature, between spirit and matter, mind and body, subject and object, intellect and soul, and, perhaps most fundamentally, between masculine and feminine — to discover a deeper unitive consciousness.[52]

In passing, but perhaps importantly at this point, it must be said that, if taken from the point of view of the overthrow of patriarchy, this also fits a biblical interpretation. For according to Margaret Barker and other feminist scholars, there was a revolution in the seventh century BC in ancient Israel in which the whole tradition of Wisdom, personified as the goddess, was downgraded and replaced by the concept of Torah, Law — that is, Matriarchy was replaced by Patriarchy and Wisdom was only kept as a philosophical minority devotion. In Hebrew she was known as Chokmah, in Greek as Sophia. She was marginalized from that time except for a brief restoration in the second century BC, when she returned to lead a precarious, fugitive life among the Essenes and Therapeutae and may, through them, have been a great influence on Jesus.

She was impossible to marginalize within the Hermetic tradition because she was, of course, integral to all systems of astrology and cosmology. She was also integral in symbol, as we have seen, to the Arthurian and Grail romances. Hugh Schonfield has claimed that she was worshipped by the Templars in the form of a two-headed idol called the Baphomet. This was traditionally thought to be a cover for Mahomet and the Templars were condemned for having 'gone native' among the Saracens. However, Schonfield has claimed that Baphomet was code for Sophia — the goddess of Wisdom, using gematria, the ancient system of assigning numbers to letters, as exemplified in Chapter 3, when *krateria* the cup was analysed as equivalent to the numbers 540 and 90. Using these number-letter correspondences for Sophia, with the Atbash code of reversing their order, produces the name Baphomet. This is one of the key pieces of modern scholarly evidence which has helped to clear the Templars of heresy and evil practices, and has shown them to be genuine devotees of the goddess or, to be more precise, of Chokmah-Sophia. This comes sharply into focus in *The Templar Revelation* which was, among other things, the inspiration for some of the more controversial parts of *The Da Vinci Code*.

Whether taken literally as the goddess or philosophically as the Wisdom tradition, it is easy to see how the feminine side of the three main monotheistic religions, has been suppressed by patriarchal legalism. What is not so easy is to see how, in recent times, the subtle forces of Neptune on behalf of the feminine, have undermined the credibility of Law, Torah, as a workable coercive spiritual force. There are many ways in which this is happening but one which is particularly pervasive though difficult to assess, and which is close to our theme, is that of the growing importance of the imagination in spiritual things. This has been increasingly the case, which accounts for the huge popularity of the *Narnia* books by C.S. Lewis, the *Lord of the Rings* by J.R.R. Tolkien and the *Harry Potter* books by J.K. Rowling. There have been many, many others — such as the *Earth-Sea Trilogy* by Ursula Le Guin, *The Dark is Rising* by Susan Cooper and *His Dark Materials* by Philip Pullman. The list is almost endless, which is unsurprising because we would expect this outpouring of the archetypal — the mythic, the spiritual, the transcendent, the imaginal, the numinous — before and after the 1993 Neptune-Uranus conjunction.

The closer association between fantasy and spiritual perception is only gradually being recognized by the purveyors of traditional, institutional religion. All those brought up before the 1980s have found this a difficult transition, as they were educated and steeped in an educational system with a strong Saturnine content, since Saturn as the old ruler of Aquarius and of Capricorn held sway with a heavy hand. Knowledge and spiritual truth for Saturn are very different from what they mean to Neptune.

Nevertheless, the process of the Neptunian corrosion of Saturnine girders began as long ago as the discovery of Neptune in 1846. It helped George MacDonald to move away from the Saturnine restrictions of Church education and dry theology to the more exciting world of fantasy. His novels have had an enormous influence down the generations and have been especially acknowledged by C.S. Lewis, whose creation of *Narnia* as a literary device, as well as a fantasy, for telling essentially Christian parables and allegories, was taken directly from MacDonald's *Phantastes* and other novels. The genealogy of MacDonald's influence has been traced by many literary commentators and by none with greater charm than by Marion Lochhead in *The Renaissance of Wonder.* They lead on to the celebrated group of Oxford writers who called themselves 'The Inklings' and whose most famous members were Charles Williams, C.S. Lewis and J.R.R. Tolkien. These, and especially Tolkien, have spawned another generation of fantasy writers, even as Tolkien, himself, through the success of his films, is now enjoying his third generation of fans and admirers. The extreme youth of these — that is, younger school teenagers, compared with the first fans, mostly twenty-something hippies — indicates that despite his own inability to assess himself in terms of his popularity or lack of it, he has increasingly appealed to those for whom the imaginative reality of his creations has largely come to replace spiritual education in any formal or traditional sense. This is even the case with Harry Potter in so much as J.K. Rowling's works are easier to read and contain a lighter touch. The extent to which she is read, particularly by a generation for whom films have largely replaced books, is phenomenal. There are those now in their late teens who have actually learnt to read via Harry Potter. Harry Potter, *Lord of the Rings* and *Narnia,* have been their literary staple, their spiritual and mythological culture.

The whole upsurge of this fantasy writing was sparked off in the run up to, and during, the Neptune-Uranus conjunction of 1993, and by the enhanced Uranian and Neptunian energies as outlined above. This conjunction took place in Capricorn which indicates that it is no passing craze or fashion. As it has been growing for many years, so it is likely to stay for as long as the energies, as described above, hold sway. Capricorn is the sign of government, which might mean that it is going to continue to take centre stage in the national consciousness. We claimed earlier that the Neptune-Uranus conjunction in 452 in Leo the king, coming at the zenith of Gemini, Merlin's sign, was enough to manifest the personification of Arthur's Excalibur. Perhaps in this democratic age we are in the process of seeing the emergence of a whole Round Table of Arthurian and Merlinesque personifications! The notion of 'spin,' so strong in government, is full of Neptunian illusion, as is image and performance. Yet it would appear that even the young know the difference between being conned by politicians and recognizing the deeper 'truth' of fantasy and mythology. There also seems to be more integrity, more 'truth,' more spirit in the fantasy world of Narnia, the

Fig.45 Michael Scott's grave in Melrose Abbey

Fig.46 Melrose Abbey

Hobbit and Hogwarts, than some of the racist stories of the Bible or the often boring sermons in church. For many young people, and those not so young, fantasy has taken the place of traditional forms of Church and education. If that's a shame, as for many traditionalists it is, then perhaps the combined forces of Neptune and Uranus should be blamed. In that sense we are all victims of the Age change and epoch change whether we like it or not.

In recent years, as a regular train traveller between London Kings Cross and Edinburgh Waverley, I have become convinced that Platform $9^3/_4$ must herald the alternative route to Scotland. I cannot say exactly what this route is but the Hogwarts Express goes through country which, with its mountains, lakes (lochs) and bad weather, must be somewhere in the Highlands. Likewise, many of the staff of Hogwarts seem to me to have a distinctly Scottish flavour. However, the tradition which it takes me back to is not so much the Highlands as the Lowlands, to be precise the Borders. The tradition of Border magic, which I believe comes to life again at Hogwarts, is that of Michael Scott, the famous magician of the late twelfth and early thirteenth centuries, who was immortalized in the early nineteenth century through Sir Walter Scott's poem, *The Lay of the Last Minstrel.* He was the mysterious scholar who learnt his magic in Arab lands and became court astrologer to European kings before coming home, working many wonders and eventually being buried at Melrose Abbey. Or was he? Or did he? Was he a magician at all? Was he buried at Melrose? Was his magic book buried with him? Was he exhumed centuries later in order for his magic book to be used for dark purposes? Sir Walter Scott weaved so many fantastical stories round him that he himself seemed to take on the mantle of 'the mighty magician' and ceased to distinguish between fact and fiction. *The Lay of the Last Minstrel* in which he told the story brought Sir Walter fame and wealth and a massive tourist trade to Melrose Abbey. He was called, like Michael Scott himself, the Wizard of the North and ran his own equivalent of Hogwarts. Replace Abbotsford and Melrose with Hogwarts and Roslin Chapel and who can doubt that, geographically, we have only moved just down the road but in time we have moved one complete cycle of Neptune-Uranus conjunctions, that is, 171 years from 1821 to 1993. Actually, *The Lay of the Last Minstrel* was published in 1805 but 1821 coincided with the height of Scott's fame.

6. Michael Scott and Thomas the Rhymer

The link between the upsurge of the 'archetypal — the mythic, the spiritual, the transcendent, the imaginal, the numinous' — which Tarnas says are the distinguishing manifestations of the period around a Uranus-Neptune conjunction, has already been noted between the recent one of 1993 and the previous one in 1821. More does not need to be said. Nevertheless, it is worth noting to what extent history *does* repeat itself in the remarkable fame that came to Sir Walter Scott as a result of his mythologizing, fantasizing, romanticizing, or however one views his work. His reputed passion for history and antiquarian studies made his 'economy with the truth' all the more effective. Like Dan Brown, he could claim 'all descriptions of artwork, architecture, documents and secret rituals in this novel are accurate' and because he was known for serious historical scholarship, his departures into fantasy were received with a degree of both seriousness and the shock of incredulity. If we take for instance his description of the Gothic ruins of Melrose Abbey:

> If thou would'st view fair Melrose aright,
> Go visit it by the pale moonlight;
> For the gay beams of lightsome day
> Gild, but to flout, the ruins grey.
> When the broken arches are black in night,
> And each shafted oriel glimmers white;
> When the cold light's uncertain shower
> Streams on the ruin'd central tower;
> When buttress and buttress, alternately,
> Seem fram'd of ebon and ivory;
> When silver edges the imagery,
> And the scrolls that teach thee to live and die;
> When distant Tweed is heard to rave,
> And the owlet to hoot o'er the dead man's grave,
> Then go — but go alone the while —

Michael Scott's
Tomb.

> Then view St. David's ruin'd pile;
> And, home returning, soothly swear,
> Was never scene so sad and fair![53]

It is easy to forget that this romantic portrait of Melrose Abbey brought a massive tourist trade and inspired a number of romantic landscapes by nineteenth-century artists.

We could at least claim that Scott was scenically accurate within the limits of the romantic genre of pleasing horror. It is precisely this which enables him to subtly weave his fantasy under cover of the moonlight. A few stanzas further on we move into one of the most dramatic scenes of *The Lay of the Last Minstrel,* in which a knight under the orders of Lady Branksome, a sixteenth-century landed border widow, exhumes the body of Michael Scott the ancient wizard, in order to steal his famous magic book, with which his mistress hopes to cast evil, vengeful spells. With the help of an old monk he lifts the lid of the grave in the moonlight:

> Before their eyes the Wizard lay,
> As if he had not been dead a day.
> His hoary beard in silver roll'd,
> He seem'd some seventy winters old;
> A palmer's amice wrapped him round,
> With a wrought Spanish baldric bound,
> Like a pilgrim from beyond the sea:
> His left hand held his Book of Might;
> A silver cross was in his right;

> Then Deloraine, in terror, took
> From the cold hand the Mighty Book,
> With iron clasp'd, and with iron bound:
> He thought, as he took it, the dead man frown'd;
> But the glare of the sepulchral light,
> Perchance, had dazzled the warrior's sight.[54]

Fig.47 Effigy of Michael Scott in Melrose Abbey

The exact point when romantic exaggeration moves into fantasy passes and the place where Scott, the Wizard of the North, starts to weave his magic is not noticed. We are in the hands of a consummate story-teller who can tell a ripping yarn, which moves in and out of historical fact in a way that compares favourably with his contemporary successors. The inclusion of a goblin-page as an important character, who later steals Michael Scott's Book and uses it out of pure mischief to lure Lady Branksome's infant son into the woods, only adds to the effectiveness of the medieval magical atmosphere. It evokes the world, which has come alive again in recent years at Hogwarts, to such an extent that one has come to tremble at the responsibility resting on the shoulders of the Professor of The Defence against the Dark Arts. It is no wonder that the post has always had such disastrous repercussions for its incumbent.

Sir Walter Scott did nothing to help the average Muggle disentangle historical fiction from the fabulous stories about Michael Scott's wizardry. In his 'historical notes' he listed the most bizarre tales. The fabled Michael is said to have feasted his friends with dishes brought by spirits from the royal kitchens of France and Spain. His embassy to France, alone on the back of a coal-black demon steed, is also narrated by Sir Walter at length, as is the episode where he brought the French king to his knees as a result of the stamping of his horse's hooves, which made the bells of Notre Dame ring and then caused the tower of the palace to fall down.

But Michael Scott's reputation as a magician had already been established long before Sir Walter embellished it. Even by the generation after his death, in the thirteenth century, he had appeared in Dante's *Divine Comedy* among the magicians and soothsayers in the eighth circle of Hell (*Inferno*, canto XX, 115–17). Boccaccio represents him in the same character and Giovanni Pico della Mirandola criticizes him severely in his work against astrology. Nevertheless, Sir Walter did much to make sure that this reputation was enhanced, especially for instance in his attribution of the cleaving of the Eildon hills in three:

> And, Warrior, I could say to thee
> The words that cleft Eildon hills in three,
> And bridled the Tweed with a curb of stone:
> But to speak them were a deadly sin;

> And for having but thought them my heart within,
> A treble penance must be done.[55]

This reputation has been so perpetuated that fact and fiction seem to be still inseparable. For instance, in a recent children's fantasy television series a good wizard comes to life again to help guide a motherless child to the book of forbidden knowledge. Even when Sir Walter purports to give a serious historical note about the real Scott, he claims without a shadow of doubt that he 'was one of the ambassadors sent to bring the Maid of Norway to Scotland upon the death of Alexander III.' This is also pure fabrication because Alexander III died in 1286 but Scott died no later than 1236. Unless of course Sir Walter believed he was like Count Saint Germain and had a miraculous longevity! However, despite having effectively mythologized Scott out of normal history books, it must be conceded that Sir Walter does pay his passing, though rather reluctant, respects to the genuine history behind the legend:

> He was a man of much learning, chiefly acquired in foreign countries. He wrote a commentary upon Aristotle, printed at Venice in 1496; and several treatises upon natural philosophy, from which he appears to have been addicted to the abstruse studies of judicial astrology, alchymy, physiognomy and chiromancy. Hence he passed among his contemporaries for a skilful magician.[56]

As far as he goes, Sir Walter is right, although he shows his bias against the real man by calling his erudition an 'addiction to abstruse studies' and telling us so little about them. In recent years the Wizard seems to be at long last emerging from the mythological notoriety and historical obscurity into which Sir Walter cast him. At the risk of spoiling a good story, it is germane to our quest for Merlin to help Michael throw off his magical mask and reveal his historical identity. An outline of his life and works will show us that, in his unusual case, truth is stranger than fiction and opens the way to an unexpected and profound mystery.

The real Michael Scott

For those who have bothered to find out, and it's not hard, the real
Michael Scott was, and is, known as a medieval mathematician and
astrologer. He was born in Scotland in 1175 and studied philosophy,
mathematics, theology and astrology in Oxford and Paris. We know that
he also became an ordained priest because Pope Honorius III wrote to
Archbishop Stephen Langton in 1224 urging him to confer an English
benefice on Scott, and actually nominated him as archbishop of Cashel
in Ireland. Scott's passion was for scholarship so he turned this down
although he does seem to have held benefices in Italy from time to
time.

From Paris, Scott went to Bologna and, after a short stay at the court
of the Emperor Frederick II in Palermo, he went to Toledo. There he
learnt Arabic, which opened him up to the world of Arab commentaries
on Aristotle and the original works of Avicenna and Averroës, and there
he began his scholarly career as a translator. Along with many other
scholars, Frederick II attracted him to his court and commissioned him
to make a fresh translation of Aristotle and his Arab commentators, from
Arabic to Latin. His translations of the *Historia Animalium, De Anima*
and *De Coelo* became famous and are still in existence, as are his commentaries on Averroes.

In the Middle Ages both the Emperor Frederick II and Averroës had
a mixed reputation in the Christian world of Northern Europe, which
may have contributed to the legend that soon enveloped Scott's name.
However, his own books had much more to do with it, dealing as they do
almost exclusively with astrology, alchemy and the occult sciences generally. It wasn't surprising that he came to be thought of as a Professor
of the Dark Arts. However, such was the level of popular superstition
and suspicion of the more unfamiliar aspects of Islamic scholarship,
which was seeping into northern Europe from Spain at that time, that it is
easy to see how it would have been understandable for Scott's academic
versatility and brilliance to have been caricatured and given a negative
spin.

As we have mentioned earlier, there was what can only be called a
Renaissance of learning taking place in North-West Europe during the
twelfth and thirteenth centuries as a result of the impact of Islamic learning. It took time for acceptance to take place; it was learning which was

often initially greeted with suspicion because it came from the enemy, the Islamic infidels, who themselves were rejected and remained 'the other,' who were also considered the purveyors of a false religion and of certain false academic subjects, or ones which were at least problematic. Among these were astrology, alchemy and, at least for a time, Aristotle, who was considered suspect in a world dominated by Christian Platonism. While the general attitude to Aristotle changed during the thirteenth century, that towards astrology and alchemy largely did not and they continued to be regarded with suspicion until the dawn of the modern scientific revolution led to their complete rejection. Thus, Michael Scott's name became associated with this traditional suspicion and rejection of what were thought of as the dark arts, known popularly as Black Magic. Hence he remains to this day the Wizard of the North.

Yet this demonization of the so-called 'occult' by mainstream Christianity and science over the centuries has left us today with the feeling that, while it has been understandable, something has been lost, that while magic can be dangerous it is not always 'black,' and that lives without any magic are ultimately boring and fall prey to the meaninglessness of a worldview, which is dominated by value being given exclusively to the rational, the measurable and the economic.

Hence those, such as Sir Walter Scott, who can convince us that Michael Scott's magic, though dangerous, is nevertheless basically white not black and can weave a story round him that grips our imagination, are to be congratulated. Likewise J.K. Rowling, despite vicious excoriations from the anti-magic-of-any-kind-Christian-fundamentalist opposition, is to be praised, as are *Lord of the Rings* and *Narnia,* and many other masterpieces of fantasy, for they nourish our imagination, which has been starved for a long time by the imaginative sterility, by the conventional wisdom of our religious and secular worldview.

Michael Scott and Adelard of Bath

It is striking how similar Michael Scott's life is to that of Adelard of Bath. Like Michael Scott, Adelard spent much of his life abroad and became a famous translator of classical texts from Arabic to Latin. They differ to the extent that Adelard's translations, including his astrology, received widespread recognition whereas, seventy-five years later, Scott's did not, at least not his 'occult' texts. But they do seem to be very much on a par as regards the impact of their esoteric studies on the cognoscenti of their day. For it looks very much as if Scott's magic book, his *Book of Might,* played the same symbolic role as Adelard's emerald ring, for those who knew. Scott was born twenty-five years after Geoffrey of Monmouth died, so could not in any way have had an influence on the creation of his Arthurian or Merlin oeuvre. None the less it is possible to see both Adelard and Michael as examples, as exemplars, of the pervasive and continuing influence of the hermetic tradition.

It was shown in Chapter 2, that the whole of the Arthurian and Grail literature can be interpreted as a symbolic system in which the hermetic axiom 'as above, so below' sheds much light on each and every narrative component. While it is obvious that Michael Scott could have had no influence on Geoffrey of Monmouth, it is nevertheless significant that he lived through the time of the composition of the great Grail romances of the turn of the twelfth and thirteenth centuries, particularly those of Robert de Boron and Wolfram von Eschenbach. It could also be significant that during his studies in Europe as a young man, he learnt Arabic at Toledo, for this opened up his life to the world of Aristotle, Islamic astrology and alchemy. The reason why this could have been significant and indeed relevant to us, is that in 1208, when Scott was thirty-three, Wolfram von Eschenbach published his famous reworking of Chrétien de Troyes' *Perceval* (called *Parzival).* In this von Eschenbach claimed that Chrétien had got the story wrong and that he was telling it the way it really was. One important aspect, which he claimed was unique to his retelling, was that the story of the Grail in its prime version had been found by a certain Master Kyot 'lying all neglected in a corner of Toledo.' It had been written in Arabic, which Master Kyot had had to learn in order to translate it.

It could only have been a coincidence, nevertheless it is odd that a man who has been branded a Wizard in Scotland for eight hundred years, should have been learning Arabic in order to translate important Islamic magical texts in Toledo as a brilliant young scholar, round about that very time. It is also odd that from that day to this, scholars and romancers have been debating what exactly Wolfram von Eschenbach meant by the *graal,* even as they have been debating the exact identity of Michael Scott. It is also most strange that just down the road from Michael's final resting place, in Roslin, is the famous medieval chapel that has for centuries been associated with the secret hiding place of the Grail and which, today, is being flooded by thousands of tourists eager to experience it as the Grail chapel of the *The Da Vinci Code*.

It is particularly tempting to make more of these connections, dubious though the likelihood of their historical veracity may be. This is even more the case when we remember that it was not merely the story of the Grail as such that was found in a forgotten Arabic manuscript in a neglected corner of Toledo, but of the Grail *in the stars*. It was the story of the Grail *in the stars* that Master Kyot found in Toledo. It was through the agency of a heathen astrologer called Flegetanis, who said that he could see 'hidden secrets in the constellations.' He declared that 'there was a thing called the Gral, whose name he read in the stars without more ado.'[57] Was Michael Scott's *Book of Magic* a book of Grail Magic? Was it, to be more precise, a

Fig.48 The Eildon hills

book of Star Grail Magic? Knowing his reputation for astrological studies and alchemy, the cap would certainly fit and so would the not so unexpected presence of a brilliant young Scottish scholar lurking in the shadows of this tantalizing but important story because, at that time, Toledo's interfaith scholarly reputation was attracting students from all over Europe.

Be that as it may I still cannot find any confirmation that any of these connections are more than possibilities or speculation. But perhaps it is not possible to find any in a matter which is so thin on hard historical facts. The Michael Scott trail has been so obscured by the tangled magical overlay that 'now you never could tell, there was once a way through the woods.' This is even more the case with Thomas the Rhymer than with Michael Scott. Their lives overlapped by fifteen years, the latter dying circa 1235 and the former being born circa 1220, and both were extant in Scotland within sight of the Eildon hills. The latter was known as a magician and the former as a rhyming prophet. Yet no hard historical fact or tradition links them together. The only name to which both have been likened is that of Merlin, the latter being called 'the Merlin of Scotland' and the former being likened to Merlin the prophet since the Middle Ages, as in Berlington's couplet:

> Marvellous Merlin, that many men of tells,
> And Thomas's sayings comes all at once.[58]

The absence of any hard evidence with which to link Michael Scott and Thomas the Rhymer is offset, to a considerable extent, by the fact that they have both been likened to Merlin. This is strange because this link is not confirmed by any substantial evidence, only by tradition. Yet this only has to be mentioned for it to be easily accepted. It stands out clearly as if Merlin needs no historical verification. For he is universally recognizable and recognized as an archetypal prophetic-magical character. It is almost as though he has substantial existence yet is also out of historical time. And indeed, this is how he is generally reckoned to be. This is why we have been able to talk about the return of the Merlinesque today in such characters as Gandalf and Dumbledore. So it was with Michael Scott and even more with Thomas the Rhymer. It was recognized in them and particularly the latter, that Merlin had lived again. There was no mention of reincarnation, only that they were like Merlin in many obvious ways.

*Fig.49 Thomas the Rhymer's
Castle at Ercildoune*

Thomas the Rhymer

There is much less known about Thomas the Rhymer than Michael
Scott, and in Sir Walter Scott's notes there is little that is definite and
next to no fabulous tales. It does seem certain that in 1220 his birth-
place and estate was at Ercildoune, today called Earlston, and that his
name was Thomas Learmont of Ercildoune; that he had a son of the
same name who divested himself of the family property to the convent
of the Trinity at Soltra and that Thomas Senior died circa 1297. While
his life is very thin on detail, his prophecies, or prophecies attributed
to him, were collected soon after his death and reappeared at intervals
during the following centuries. He became famous during his lifetime
by predicting the tragic death of King Alexander III the night before
the King died, on March 18, 1286. He also predicted the Battle of
Bannockburn, the Jacobite uprisings and the Union of the Crowns of
Scotland and England. This latter in a strange way linked his name
with Merlin because his prophecy foretold that when the Powsail burn

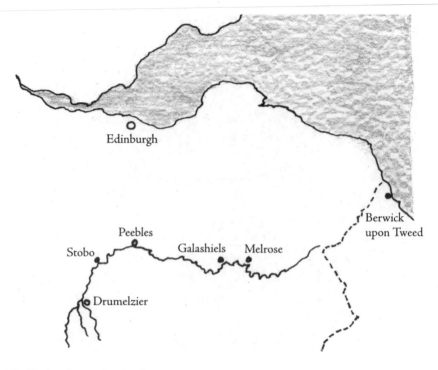

Fig.50 South-east Scotland

Fig.51 Altar stone where Merlin was baptized, Stobo

Fig.52 Merlin's stone, Drumelzier

overflowed into the River Tweed at Merlin's grave, the crowns would be united. Following the tradition of Merlin Lailoken, not that of Geoffrey of Monmouth, Merlin was said to have wandered the woods in his distracted state at Drumelzier near Stobo until he was baptized by St Kentigern and then suffered a threefold death in the Tweed. His grave is said to be marked either with a standing stone or a thorn tree. Sir Walter Scott tells the story:

> The grave of Merlin is pointed out at Drumelzier, in Tweedale, beneath an aged thorn-tree. On the east side of the churchyard the brook, called Pausayl falls into the Tweed; and the following prophecy is said to have been current concerning their union: —
>
> > When Tweed and Pausayl join at Merlin's grave,
> > Scotland and England shall one monarch have.

Fig.53 Where the Powsail Burn and the River Tweed meet, Drumelzier

On the day of the coronation of James VI, the Tweed
accordingly over-flowed, and joined the Pausayl at the
prophet's grave.[59]

Scott's notes on Thomas the Rhymer expatiate on the possible source
of his prophetic muse and these include a certain nun of Haddington.
Yet most over the centuries have assumed they came from his own gift
while, amongst the mass of ordinary people, he has always been considered the mouthpiece of the Fairy Queen. This is because according to the
famous ballad for which he is remembered, he made a mysterious visit
with her to Fairyland:

> Whatever doubts, however, the learned might have as to the
> source of the Rhymer's prophetic skill, the vulgar had no
> hesitation to ascribe the whole to the intercourse between
> the bard and the Queen of Faëry. The popular tale bears that
> Thomas was carried off, at an early age, to the Fairy Land,
> where he acquired all the knowledge which afterwards
> made him so famous. After seven years residence, he was

Fig.54 Merlin baptized by St Kentigern, Stobo Kirk

permitted to return to the earth, to enlighten and astonish his countrymen by his prophetic powers; still however remaining bound to return to his royal mistress, when she should intimate her pleasure. Accordingly, while Thomas was making merry with his friends in the Tower of Ercildoune, a person came running in and told, with marks of fear and astonishment, that a hart and a hind had left the neighbouring forest, and were, composedly and slowly parading the street of the village. The prophet instantly arose, left his habitation and followed the wonderful animals to the forest, whence he was never seen to return. According to the popular belief, he still 'drees his weird' in Fairyland and is one day expected to revisit earth. In the meantime his memory is held in the most profound respect.[60]

After such a story, it isn't surprising that Sir Walter felt he could take liberties with the fabulous stories about Michael Scott. Compared even with Michael's magic black flying horse or the cleaving of the Eildons into three, this tale is something else. Since it comes down to us as a well-known fairy tale we have felt that we have not had to understand it. We have learnt to accept it as one of the best fairy stories of all time and to reject it as anything else. Yet in the light of our attempt to interpret the Grail stories in hermetic terms perhaps we can see through the symbolism to some inner truth.

In the strange journey which Thomas makes on horseback with the Fairy Queen, he is shown three roads, one is the narrow road of righteousness, one is the broad path of wickedness and the third is the bonnie road to fair Elfland, which is the one they must take. Can we not legitimately interpret this as the place, the *locus,* where three roads meet, the archetypal 'way' of Hermes, and the road to fair Elfland, like the Buddha's 'middle way,' being the path which leads to enlightenment?

Then they ride on through mighty rivers, then all goes dark with no sun or moon. Then the darkness deepens: 'It was mirk mirk night, and there was nae stern light, And they waded through red blude to the knee.' They went through a time of great darkness which eventually gave way to rivers of blood. Now this is so graphic and so much like fantasy that it is easy not to ascribe any actual meaning to it. Anything can happen in Fairy Land! But supposing it is actually attempting to describe something that actually happened, like a shamanic journey or an out-of-body experience.

Supposing that behind all the fantastic phantasmagoria of the Fairy genre it is relating something that is recognizable in spiritual terms.

Thomas and the Fairy Queen next come to a 'garden green,' which in Robin Williamson's modern rendering reads 'they rode out into a green and misty landscape.' This more romantic rendition has a resonance, which for me is reminiscent of the emerald light seen by the Sufi mystics during their out-of-body experiences, in the midst of deep cosmic darkness (see Chapter 3). Could the absence of sun or moon and the 'mirk mirk night' where there was 'nae stern light,' which preceded the 'green and misty landscape,' be the equivalent of the Sufi's experience of the *visio smaragdina*, the vision of the emerald rock, the ultimate goal of the Sufis' mystic journey? It is worth entertaining this possibility because we are attempting to answer the question: what exactly is this extraordinary story telling us; what is it about?

If a Sufi comparison were made, then it would be consistent with the hermetic symbolism which we have already found fits much of the otherwise obscure symbolism of the Grail stories. It would explain and render intelligible the 'magic' which surrounds the figure of Michael Scott, just as it did for Adelard of Bath.

If we were bold enough to explore this comparison a little further, then it would be important to remember that this was the period during which the Sufi masters were experiencing the Great Bear as an esoteric entity which communicated with them. It was also the time, circa 1204 onwards, during which the great mystic philosopher Ibn Arabi was having his meetings with other world beings, particularly with one known in the Islamic world as *Khidr*, whose name means the Green One, sometimes 'the Verdant One' and who, according to Henry Corbin's description of him, has characteristics which are strangely reminiscent of Merlin.[61] He is the one who personifies the Other World vision of the Emerald light. It is likely that Michael Scott, during his studies in Spain, knew a great deal about Ibn Arabi and his experiences of *Khidr*. It is even possible that his translations of occult, alchemical texts, contained some reference to him because, like Averroes and Avicenna, Ibn Arabi's Sufi writings and his experiences were famous at that very time. This spiritual world would be almost entirely unknown to the spiritually remote and 'different' Scots, yet something of the same spirit might have been present in the northern tradition of the Fairy Otherworld and have been brilliantly reactivated to produce this powerful indigenous expression.

The mystic experience, which one way or another must have been at the core of the reality behind Thomas the Rhymer, was later in the century, yet it was not that much later, and could have easily been under the same astrological influences. These, as we have already mentioned, were chronologically close to the Grail stories of Robert de Boron and Wolfram von Eschenbach and suggested the possible connection between Michael Scott and the story of the Grail in the stars that was found in Toledo. Perhaps this comparison should not be pressed too far and yet, far-fetched though it might already seem, it is otherwise odd to find so many Islamic Sufi and Hermetic connections coming so close in the person of Michael Scott, to this late flowering of what we could call Grail literature.

From the point of view of the grand trine of the Scottish Merlin as outlined in the last chapter, the story of Thomas the Rhymer fits exactly. If we say that the Otherworld journey which he describes took place shortly before he died, as is implied by his final disappearance to Fairyland around

Fig.55 Thomas the Rhymer with Alexander III and the Maid of Norway, Scottish National Portrait Gallery

1297, then this trines almost precisely with 575 and the fateful Battle of Arderydd, as described in Chapter 4. It also trines with 2017, which is a few years into the future. It is extraordinary that, in the historical frieze of famous Scottish characters in the Scottish Portrait Gallery, by John Hole, Thomas the Rhymer, unlike Michael Scott, has not been forgotten. He has been remembered as an important figure for he commands the section between Alexander III and the Maid of Norway (see Figure 55). He stands full length, is playing his harp and singing, as he did, under the inspiration of the Fairy Queen. The true identity of the Fairy Queen is of course the Goddess of the land for the fairies are the demoted gods and goddesses of ancient times. The goddess has many names and in Celtic lands she is usually called Bride. In this study we have called her Artemis because of her particular association with the Great Bear and the moon. He is still singing about his mystical shamanic experience, his Sufi Other-world journey, his *visio smaragdina* with her, of how he returned for seven years to tell his people about their true nature for he, as True Thomas, couldn't tell a lie and of how, one full moon, the fairy god and goddess called for him in the form of a hart and a hind from the forest.

In a few years time the influence of Neptune and of Uranus will have increased and those who had sought their counterfeit spiritual 'highs' from drugs will be beginning to turn towards genuine mystical quest. At that time we will be moving from an approximate to an exact trine with the Otherworld journey of Thomas the Rhymer, the Sufi encounters of Ibn Arabi with *Khidr* and Merlin's encounter with the healing waters of the Goddess, seven hundred and twenty years before. It will be a time when the reality of similar supernatural experiences will change many lives and reveal the universal and enduring truths, which lie behind the gripping stories known today as 'fantasy.'

In anticipation of this, and as a reminder of the final scene of the story of True Thomas, the last few verses will bring to a close this essay on our Merlin tradition in star lore and its recurrence in the patterns of history:

> A hart and hind pace side by side,
> As white as snow on Fairnalie.
>
> Beneath the moon with gesture proud
> They stately move and slow;
> Nor scare they at the gathering crowd,
> Who marvel as they go.

The hart and hind approach'd the place
As lingering yet he stood;
And there, before Lord Douglas' face,
With them he cross'd the flood.
Some said to hill, and some to glen,
Their wondrous course had been;
But ne'er in haunts of living men
Again was Thomas seen.[62]

Postscript

The picture of True Thomas following the hart and hind by moonlight across the flooded river Leader and into the forest, makes a dramatic and appropriate finale to this weird story. Yet it is not true to say that 'ne'er in haunts of living men, Again was Thomas seen.' For quite apart from the cycle of Merlin reappearances in other guises, which we have been considering, there is one story of Thomas' reappearance which is still alive in the vicinity of the Eildons and is well known today. His continuing association with the figure of Merlin is implied by the revelation that the Eildon Hills contain a large cave where King Arthur is sleeping with his knights.

This story concerns a horse-dealer named Canonbie Dick who was stopped by an old man one night on nearby Bowden Moor. The man bought two of his horses and said he would buy more the next day. This duly took place after which Canonbie Dick proposed sealing the bargain with a drink, whereupon the old man led him to a cave in the Eildon Hills and revealed himself to be the prophet Thomas the Rhymer. In the cave Dick saw stables of black horses with a knight in black armour sleeping beside each one. He also saw a table with a sword and a horn on it. Thomas offered Dick the choice of blowing the horn or drawing the sword first, prophesying that he who made the right choice would be 'King of all Britain.' Beryl Beave tells the rest of the story in *Scotland — Myths and Legends*:

> Dick made the wrong choice and blew the horn. Immediately,
> a great voice proclaimed:
>   'Woe the coward that ever he was born,
>   Who did not draw the sword before he blew the horn.'

> A whirlwind then cast Dick from the cave, injuring him
> so badly that he lived only long enough to tell his story to
> the shepherds who discovered him.[63]

Over the years there have been many expeditions to discover the entrance to the cave of Arthur and his knights. It has never been found which isn't surprising because most people have taken this whole story to be a complete fabrication. Yet it is strange that despite the suspicion that we are dealing here with a complete fiction, the subject of King Arthur and his knights, of Merlin and of Thomas the Rhymer, has come alive again in recent years from a completely new and serious scholarly source.

In *Arthur and the Lost Kingdoms,* Borders historian Alistair Moffat makes a very convincing case for the historical Arthur having been a prince and brilliant cavalry general of the post-Roman Borders tribe, the Gododdin. Since my book has been primarily about Merlin, not Arthur, and about star lore, not history, it is not appropriate to examine Moffat's thesis in detail. However, his research into the history-legend of Thomas the Rhymer helps to conclude this essay on a suitably ambiguous note:

> Thomas visited the Celtic Otherworld, entering it through
> the portal traditionally revered by their priests. He went on
> Samhuinn Eve when any barriers between men and the super-
> natural were lowered. And he came back with the gift of the
> second sight, with the magic of a P-Celtic holy man.[64]

Like his foretelling of the death of Alexander III, many of the Rhymer's prophecies are pessimistic. Yet Moffat says that those contained in what scholars call his 'Third Fythe' are more optimistic and concern the return of Arthur:

> In summary he predicts the return of Arthur who sleeps
> with his knights under the Eildon Hill. There is, he writes,
> 'a good time coming' when 'the kind conqueror' will
> ride from the west and defeat the Saxons before uniting
> Britain.[65]

Moffat says that 'The Romance of Thomas' spread quickly throughout Scotland. In the Highlands he became a heroic, mythic figure known as Tomas Reumhair, or Thomas the Wanderer. He became the transmitter of the Arthurian hope in a Merlinesque fashion:

> 'The leadership of the Gael in his customary step, will fall to a champion of the warlord of Britain.' Attributed to Thomas, this sounds like a repetition of a Merlin prophecy of the emergence of someone very like Arthur. What is clearly traceable is the transmission through the cult of Thomas of this sort of story in the Gaidhealtachd of the highlands of Scotland. Echoes survived in tales of Thomas or his shade at markets searching for good horses, clearly with warfare in mind. At some point the prophet supplanted the prophesied and Thomas became Arthur .... the phenomenon of Thomas the Rhymer shows how the Celtic magic of the Eildons kept its power long after the fires ceased to be lit on its summit.[66]

From Moffat's very thorough research we can assume that by the time Canonbie Dick had his weird encounter with Thomas the Rhymer he had turned into Arthur searching for good horses with which to replenish his warband.

We can also assume that, for the serious historian who is not biased against the full spectrum of historical data by modern prejudices against the part which legend, folklore and myth play in understanding the past, a clear distinction between each of these categories and fantasy is not easy to draw. Finding the balance between them with regard to Thomas the Rhymer would appear to be as difficult as we have found it to be for Merlin, Arthur, the Knights of the Round Table and the Grail. Perhaps introducing star lore as an interpretative category would only serve to muddy the waters of clear historical judgement. Nevertheless, returning to that theme, it is strange that at a time when the dry bones of academic historiography still rattle loud, the more balanced and liberal interpretation of the Thomas the Rhymer material by Alistair Moffat could itself perhaps be seen as an expression of the upsurge of 'the archetypal — the mythic, the imaginal, the numinous,' which Richard Tarnas says comes at the time of a Neptune-Uranus conjunction, which has been the leitmotif of this book. This could perhaps also be said of his relocation of Arthur to the Borders from Tintagel and of Camelot from Cadbury Castle to Roxburgh. It may not be doing him or any other serious historian of these mysterious matters any favours to observe that all that he claims for Arthur fits the English

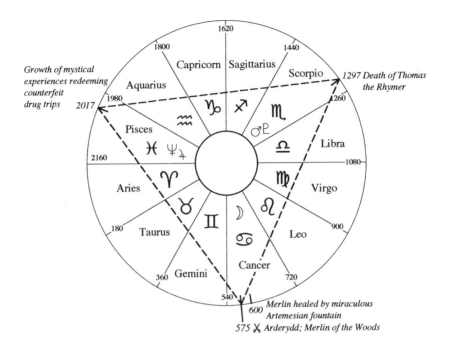

Fig.56 Grand trine of Thomas the Rhymer

grand trine in Air signs as outlined in previous chapters. However, that this is indeed the case could also be seen as significant as anything else claimed for the tradition of hermetic symbolism which springs from star lore. Yet it must also be noted that, as outlined in Chapter 3, the grand trine of Arthur took place in the fifth and twelfth centuries, with his 'rebirth' in the poetry of Tennyson in mid-nineteenth century. The Arthur who now seems to be returning to Scotland is not that English Arthur whose Merlin was Merlin Emrys. He would appear to be a Caledonian Arthur whose Merlin is the Caledonian Merlin of the Woods but who the historical process has not yet seen manifest. He is the Arthur into whom Thomas the Rhymer had changed by the time he had his encounter with Canonbie Dick in the cave in the Eildons. This is the Arthur of the Celtic Otherworld journey. The Arthur who, as Thomas the Rhymer, leads to the shamanic victory over the contemporary counterfeit Neptunian drug trips; who leads to the mystical marriage with the feminine spirit of the Goddess and whose exact trine of 720 years takes place in a few years time.

Appendix: Finding Your Cosmic Birthday

The well known saying 'There's no such thing as history, only historians' is a commonplace one, not to say a cliché. Yet it is a good antidote against historians whose presuppositions are considered to be so self-evident that they do not need to be examined or assessed. As I said earlier, such were those at Oxford in my day and I would have to accept that in reaction to my negative experience there, I may have gone to the opposite extreme. For in following the historiography of Charles Carter, I have put myself on the outer fringes of what could be called history as such. This may be said to be so apparent that it could be claimed that the patterns I have discovered, based on Carter's astrological paradigm, are too subjective to have any objective value. While I would not agree with such a dismissal altogether, I would concede that this might be considered a serious limitation.

Just how much this could be true dawned on me long after I had discovered the trine relationships between the historical cycles, which I have explained above. It happened when I asked myself where my own birthday fitted into the cycle of the epochs. It wasn't hard to find because my birthday is January 24, which in astrological language is 3° Aquarius. As mentioned earlier in Carter's system, each degree is equivalent to six years so, because the epoch of Aquarius starts in 1800, 3° is equivalent to 1818 (3 × 6 = 18). My cosmic 'birthday' thus came three years after Waterloo and three years before the Neptune-Uranus conjunction, which marked the height of the Romantic movement, as Tarnas explained. This was an extraordinary revelation because, since I was a boy, I have found my cultural home in the paintings of Turner, the poetry of Wordsworth and the music of Beethoven, all of whom were big names at that time. Needless to say my *Boys' Own Paper* hero was Napoleon, not Wellington.

All this was not uncommon given the ethos of private education in the generation after the Second World War. What was not so common was that I passed my entrance exam for Oxford in English (not History) on the basis of having read Sir Walter Scott's novels — voluntarily! This was regarded as a rare achievement, which none of the interviewing dons could match! Was this because my cosmic birthday coincided with the heyday of Scott's literary output? Is this why this book has concluded with an astrological analysis of Scott and *The Lay of the Last Minstrel?* It is certainly strange to me because this was very much not the case in the first draft. I thought I had dismissed him as a tedious windbag years ago.

Some years later, when I moved on to do post-graduate studies in Theology, my unknown cosmic birthday must have been exerting an unconscious pull on me when I chose the heresy trials of the Reverend Edward Irving as my topic. These concerned an early occurrence of what are known today as 'Pentecostal phenomena' — that is, speaking in tongues and prophesying — which took place in Irving's London church between 1830 and 1832. What fascinated me about Irving was not only his early Pentecostalism but that he was also a close friend of Thomas Carlyle, a theological disciple of the poet Coleridge, and the recipient of praise from the acid wit of William Hazlitt, who swelled his congregation with many of the famous literati and politicians of the day. Indeed, I became so absorbed in the common threads moving between the thought of all these famous contemporaries that, had I known about the Neptune-Uranus conjunction of 1821, I would have realized that I was writing a commentary on Richard Tarnas because Irving began his ministry in London in 1822 as a young man of thirty and rose to fame almost immediately. Needless to say, my ignorance and prejudice was such that I was never able to identify the common factor and my supervisor said that, while it was worthwhile to bring together these disparate strands of thought, it wasn't, strictly speaking, my topic and that I should get that done first. So it still remains an unfinished manuscript.

Years later, following a very different enthusiasm for sacred or symbolic geometry in the Department of Adult Eduction at Edinburgh University, I began a project with some friends on the Cathedral of Chartres, where we attempted to crack the geometrical code of this great monument to the genius of early Gothic masons. Architectural students came to my courses and I was eventually asked to offer an honours course in 'The Rise of the Gothic' within the Department of Architecture. The upshot of this was that I was able to complete my analysis of Chartres, which was published in 2002 as *Chartres: Sacred Geometry, Sacred Space.*

The reason for mentioning all this is not to boast about my achievements but to make an observation, which is relevant to my present topic. Namely, if you take an exact trine of 720 years from 3° Aquarius at 1818 to 3° Libra you come to 1098. The extraordinary historical fact is that it was during 1098 that the Crusaders were on their way to the Holy Land, and this was the moment in history when they saw the magnificent new mosques at Diyarkbakir, Gazientep, Sürt and Bitlis for the first time. It was the following year that, after capturing Jerusalem, they saw the Aksa mosque on the Temple Mount and it was from that moment that it can be said that 'the new style' of what was later called 'Gothic' started. For the so-called Gothic pointed arch, began as an exact replica of the arches of the porch of the Aksa mosque, known as the *mukhammas* or 'fifth' arch within the Islamic tradition of sacred architecture. The process of transmission took many years but was first most beautifully expressed in the three *mukhammas* arches of the West or Royal Portal of Chartres.

Although I never made the personal connection until recently, I couldn't help noticing how the rise of the Gothic in the twelfth century was replicated almost exactly a trine of 720 years later, as was the resurgence of the Grail literature. I have put all this in the present manuscript but now I am raising the question regarding its relationship with my own cosmic birthday. Is it pure coincidence that I have been led towards fields of study which are exactly a trine apart and that I have published in both? Am I a living cosmic trine? Do I in some mysterious way carry with me an energy which relates to these two important periods of history? Going back another trine to 3° Gemini takes us to 360 plus 18 = 378 which saw the first serious revolt in Britain against the Roman rule. There is no need to attempt to fit this into a significant trine except to note that this book has been expressly concerned to quite literally 'chart,' astrologically, the trine between the post Roman Age of Arthur and that of the Gothic Grail Romances.

What emerges for me from this personal autobiography is that I have been attracted to periods of history that reflect my personal cosmic birthday. In other words, I appear to have created an interpretation of history in my own image. I, like Carter no doubt, have selected certain facts from the plethora of history and imposed a meaningful pattern on them, which may have no value beyond myself. Or have I? Is that really all I have done? If my cosmic birthday were different, would I have discovered a different, but equally meaningful pattern? If you as a reader, worked out your cosmic birthday, would you discover other trines which were meaningful to you? You may already have been critical, noting that all that I have found are trines in the elements of Air and Water. What about Fire and Earth? Surely there must be other trines there which would be meaningful to those with birthdays in Fire or Earth signs.

In order to defend myself against these legitimate criticisms and to offset the charge that I have created a history in my own image, I have now to come clean and admit that I have found other trines in Earth and Fire which may help to mitigate these charges and also to help vindicate Charles Carter's theory of cosmic epochs. They sprang very easily and obviously from architectural history, which became clear to me when studying and teaching it over the years. I was struck by the fact that most of my colleagues accepted that the peak of architectural achievement in European history was the Italian Renaissance. They were anxious to teach it and become experts in it. They took their students to study it in Rome, Florence, Venice and Urbino, and had no serious concern for Gothic. Gothic was medieval and therefore too early and too irrational. The greatness of Chartres did not appeal to them. Their students never went to Paris. The home of Gothic didn't fit their consciousness. As my Professor commented somewhat smugly 'Gothic is culture, Classical is civilization.' No wonder they gave me the Gothic slot!

I offer three charts which demonstrate that the Classical tradition of architecture and most probably of classical culture have flourished in epochs ruled primarily by the Earth signs — Taurus, Virgo and Capricorn — and secondarily by Fire epochs — Aries, Leo and Sagittarius. Let no one accuse me of Air or Water bias. This book has been about the return of Merlin, which is appropriate for an Air and a Water epoch. Merlin does not feature strongly in either Earth or Fire epochs. Other important archetypes do but must be left for another occasion. What can reasonably be deduced from this is that I am a Gothic romantic because I am an Aquarian but even that is not necessarily inevitable because there is more to each one of us than sun signs. We each have an ascendant, a moon position and stars sometimes in each house with complex patterns of aspects between them, which it is only possible for a trained astrologer to understand and interpret. So all that I say must be taken with this strict caveat. To put it simply, but very importantly, each one of us is unique and doesn't necessarily fit an obvious pattern. I do because I am *very* Aquarian having five planets, known as a 'stellium,' in Aquarius. All I have attempted to explain may be considered simplistic by astrological, as well as historical, standards. However, I have written what could be called an introduction to both, which could be thought of as important because there has been so little written which brings these two subjects together.

I now hand the whole matter over to you, the reader. From your birthday it is easy to work out your cosmic birthday and to take trines from it. If you are a Piscean and your cosmic birthday is still in the future, then go back to the equivalent degree in Scorpio and in Cancer and see if you have any trine resonances. For those of you unsure of your zodiac sun sign they are: January 20, 1° Aquarius; February 19, 1° Pisces; March 21, 1° Aries; April 20, 1° Taurus; May 21, 1° Gemini; June 21, 1° Cancer; July 23, 1° Leo; August 23, 1° Virgo; September 23, 1° Libra; October 23, 1° Scorpio; November 22, 1° Sagittarius; December 22, 1° Capricorn. If you are on the 31st of any month make it the 30th and anyway you are on the cusp so both months could be significant. Likewise February 29. The cosmic equivalent need not be precise. The inner cusp or orb is usually taken as 2° — that is, twelve years — while the outer cusp or orb can be as large as 8° — that is, 48 years. You will either see a historical connection quite quickly or not. In this epoch of pluralism, it is important for each of us to respect and be respected as an important member of the cosmic multiplicity. Fashions change; mutability is of the essence. Out of my respect for my classical colleagues, to vindicate my mentor Charles Carter and to help you find meaningful trines to your own birthday, I offer these architectural trines of the classical tradition in Earth epochs with a little in Fire.

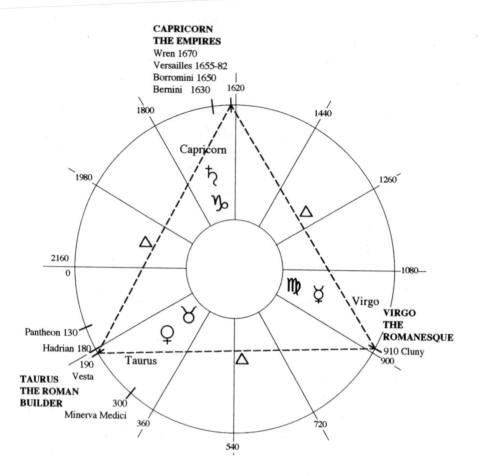

Fig.57

1. Classical architecture as a grand trine in Earth Signs

This trine is between Hadrian 180, the Temple of Vesta 190 and the
great Age of Roman Imperial building in Taurus one of whose attributes
is building. This trines with the Abbey at Cluny of 910 in Virgo which
was crucial to the rise of the Romanesque which, as its name implies,
looked back to the great Roman age. Cluny was built three times and
was the mother house for thousands of Abbeys throughout Europe. This
trines with the Classicism of the late Renaissance — 1630 Bernini, 1650
Borromini, Versailles 1655–82 and Sir Christopher Wren 1670.

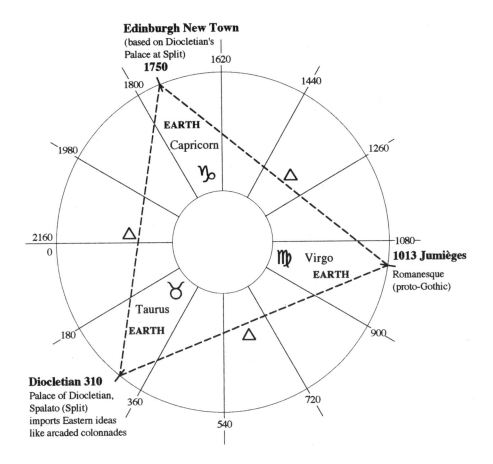

Fig.58

2. Robert Adam (1728–1792) and the Classical grand trine

The remarkable trine between Robert Adam, 1750, and the Palace of Diocletian at Split 310, is as precise and possibly as important within the Classical tradition as is that between Sens-St Denis and the Palace of Westminster in the Gothic-neo Gothic tradition, as outlined in Chapter 3. They both trine with the Abbey at Jumiéges which, although not as famous as Diocletian's Palace or Adam's Edinburgh New Town, has an important place within the history of architecture as, perhaps significantly, a marker of the transition period between the Romanesque and the Gothic.

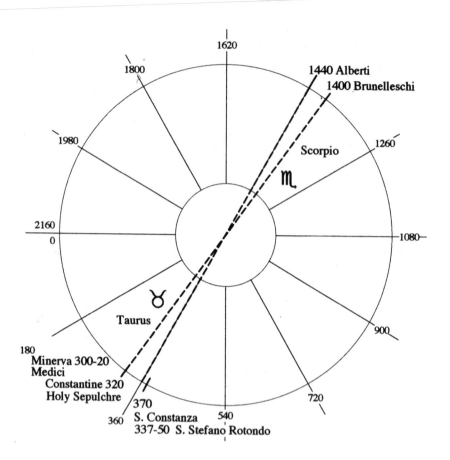

Fig.59

3. The great Classical axis: Constantine-Brunelleschi

This is not a trine, but what is called an 'opposition' in astrology of 1080 years. Oppositions can be interpreted either as energies which are opposed to each other as the name indicates, or as complementary energies which work well together. Thus it is said that Virgo is the opposite to Pisces, but is also complementary and that there are only six axes of complementary signs in astrology. Obviously the opposition formed between Brunelleschi and Alberti in late Scorpio into Sagittarius was hugely complementary to the late Taurean and early Gemini energies of the late Roman Empire. Alberti was *the number one* theorist for the Italian Renaissance and named the Roman models he based his work on. Among them were Minerva Medici 300–320, Saint Constanza 370 and Saint Stefano Rodondo 337–350.

Endnotes

Chapter 1

1. English translation from medieval Welsh of a manuscript fragment attributed to Merlin. Rendered into modern Welsh by Gareth Davies:

   Ymhen saith can mlynedd,
     byddaf'n ol gydag Arthur,
   A byddant Dynion y Gogledd yn codi.
   Welant y Gogledd tu hwnt i'r gogledd,
   A gwenu bydd Ffortiwn.

2. George Buchanan, *History of Scotland,* Vol I, Blackie, Glasgow, 1827, pp.233–34.

Chapter 2

3. Geoffrey of Monmouth, *The History of the Kings of Britain,* translated Lewis Thorpe, Penguin Books 1966, Introduction p.9.
4. Jean Markale, *Merlin, Priest of Nature,* translated Belle N.Burke, Inner Traditions 1995, p.7.
5. Charles Carter, *An Introduction to Political Astrology,* L.N. Fowler, Romford Essex 1980, p.81.
6. Geoffrey Ashe, 'Merlin in the Earliest Records' in *The Book of Merlin,* ed. R.J. Stewart, Blandford 1991, p.25.
7. Geoffrey Ashe, *op. cit.,* p.26.
8. John Michell, *City of Revelation,* Abacus 1973, p.132.
9. John Michell, *op. cit.,* p.132.
10. Geoffrey Ashe, *op. cit.,* p.35. *The White Book of Rhydderch,* was published a hundred years after Geoffrey of Monmouth but contains much material from earlier centuries.
11. Caesar, *The Conquest of Gaul,* Penguin Classics 1982, p.142.
12. Geoffrey of Monmouth, *op. cit.,* p.51.
13. Margaret Gibson, 'Adelard of Bath' in *Adelard of Bath,* ed. Charles Burnett, Warburg Institute, University of London, pp.15f.
14. Henry Corbin, *The Man of Light in Iranian Sufism,* tr. Nancy Pearson, Omega Publications, Lebanon N.Y., 1994, pp.11–13.
15. John Matthews, *The Arthurian Tradition,* Element, Shaftesbury 1989, p.28.
16. Robert de Boron, 'Perceval' in *Merlin and the Grail,* tr. Nigel Bryant, D.S. Brewer, Cambridge 2003, p.116.
17. Robert de Boron, 'Joseph of Arimathea' in *Merlin and the Grail, op. cit.,* pp.15–44.
18. See Solar Fire Astrology Program.
19. Richard Tarnas, *Prometheus the Awakener,* Spring Pubs. Woodstock, Connecticut 1995, p.122.
20. Richard Tarnas, *op. cit.,* p.123

Chapter 3

21. Michael Baigent, Richard
    Leigh and Henry Lincoln, *The
    Holy Blood and the Holy Grail,*
    Jonathan Cape 1982, Corgi
    reprint 1991, p.320.
22. *The Arthurian Encyclopedia,* ed.
    Norris J.Lacy, pp.1f.
23. Vivian E. Robson, www.winshop.
    com.au/annew/Alkes.html
24. Alfred Lord Tennyson, *Morte
    d'Arthur.*
25. Anonymous, *The Quest of the
    Holy Grail.*
26. Kenneth Clark, *The Gothic
    Revival,* John Murray, London
    1978, p.120.
27. Richard Tarnas, *Prometheus
    the Awakener,* Spring Pubs
    Woodstock CT 1995, pp.127f.
28. Nicholas Goodrich-Clarke, *The
    Occult Roots of Nazism.*
29. Alfred Lord Tennyson, *Morte
    d'Arthur.*
30. Winston Churchill, *Wartime
    Speeches.*

Chapter 4

31. Nikolai Tolstoy, *The Quest for
    Merlin,* Hamish Hamilton 1985,
    p.29
32. Geoffrey of Monmouth, *The Life
    of Merlin,* trans Basil Clarke,
    Cardiff UWP, 1973, Facsimile ed.
    Mary F.E.K. Jones, p.2.
33. Geoffrey of Monmouth, *op. cit.,*
    p.2.
34. R.J. Stewart, *Merlin: The Mystic
    Life,* Arkana, Penguin 1994,
    pp.250f.
35. Geoffrey of Monmouth, *op. cit.,*
    p.3.
36. Matthew Arnold, *The Essential

Matthew Arnold,* ed. Lionel
    Trilling, Chatto and Windus,
    London 1949, pp.140–48.
37. Geoffrey of Monmouth, *op. cit.,*
    p.3.
38. Alain Erlande-Brandenberg, *The
    Cathedral Builders of the Middle
    Ages,* Thames and Hudson,
    London 1995, p.19.
39. Geoffrey of Monmouth, *op. cit.,*
    p.10.
40. John Matthews, *Taliesin,*
    Aquarian Press, London 1991,
    p.267. Also King Arthur, Carlton,
    London 2004, p.49.
41. Robert Graves, *The Greek Myths
    I,* Penguin 1960. Graves distin-
    guishes between 'the traditional
    connexion between Artemis and
    the Great Bear' and 'Artemis
    being one more title of the Triple
    Moon-goddess.' It was at Sparta
    that 'Artemis was surnamed "The
    Lady of the Lake",' pp. 86, 84 &
    299.
42. Geoffrey Ashe, 'Merlin in the
    Earliest Records' in *The Book
    of Merlin,* ed. R.J. Stewart,
    Blandford, London 1987, p.28.
43. Michael Lynch, *Scotland, A New
    History,* Pimlico, London 1992,
    p.36.
44. Matthew Fox, *Original Blessing,*
    Bear, Sante Fe N.M. 1983, p.274.
45. William Lilly, *Christian
    Astrology,* Regulus Publishers,
    1647. p.95
46. Michael Lynch, *op. cit.*
47. Williston Walker, *A History of the
    Christian Church,* T and T Clark,
    Edinburgh 1957, p.280.

Chapter 5

48. Dan Brown, *The Da Vinci Code,* Corgi Books, 2004, p.357.
49. Nicholas Campion, *The Book of World Horoscopes,* Aquarian Press, Thorsons, Wellingborough 1988, pp.397–403, 'The Start of the Age of Aquarius.' The range of 73 possible dates starts in 1762 and ends in 3550.
50. Richard Tarnas, *Prometheus the Awakener,* Spring Pubs, Woodstock CT 1995, p.122.
51. Richard Tarnas, *op. cit.*, pp.123f.
52. Richard Tarnas, *loc. cit.*

Chapter 6

53. Scott, *Poetical Works,* edited J. Logie Robertson, OUP, London 197, p.8.
54. Scott, *Poetical Works, op. cit.*, pp.11f.
55. Scott, *Poetical Works, op. cit.*, p.10
56. Scott, *Poetical Works, op. cit.*, p.64.
57. Wolfram von Eschenbach, *Parzival,* Penguin, 1980, p.232.
58. Scott, *Poetical Works, op. cit.*, p.677.
59. Scott, *Poetical Works, loc. cit.*
60. Scott, *Poetical Works, op. cit.*, p.674.
61. Henry Corbin, *Alone with the Alone,* Princeton UP, NJ, 'The Disciple of Khidr,' pp.53–67.
62. Scott, *Poetical Works, op. cit.*, p.659.
63. Beryl Beave, *Scotland — Myths and Legends,* Lomond Books, 2005.
64. Alistair Moffat, *Arthur and the Lost Kingdoms,* Phoenix, Orion, 2000, p.45
65. Alistair Moffat, *op. cit.*, p.46
66. Alistair Moffat, *op. cit.*, p.47.

Picture Credits

Index

Gordon Strachan

The Bible's Hidden Cosmology

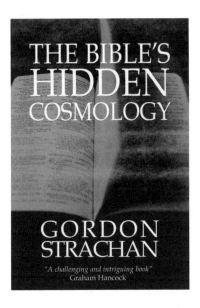

Patterns appear again and again throughout the Bible, influencing festivals and belief systems, but what are they based on? Are they incidental or deliberate?

By returning to the principles of ancient cosmology, that is, how the biblical writers viewed the universe, Gordon Strachan reveals a new understanding of the Bible. He uses the disciplines of music theory, astronomy-astrology, numerology and sacred geometry to uncover hidden wisdom and allow the ancient secrets of the Bible to shine through.

What connects Jesus to the Age of Pisces? And what clues are hidden within the Bible to alert us to the Age of Aquarius? Traditional Christianity has often obscured the importance of Christ's relationship with the cosmos, and biblical translators have constantly overlooked or ignored references in the text which might explain previously-held beliefs.

This book is a compelling whirlwind through the imagery and metaphor inherent in the Bible, giving the reader a deeper understanding of ancient wisdom traditions and a new respect for the implicit coding of the Bible.

www.florisbooks.co.uk

Gordon Strachan

Chartres: Sacred Geometry, Sacred Space

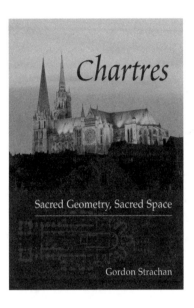

Chartres Cathedral continues to attract thousands of pilgrims after over seven hundred years. Gordon Strachan, author of *Jesus the Master Builder,* believes it is because of a unique combination of the earth energies of the ancient site, the marriage of Christian and Islamic architecture, mysticism and the skills of medieval geometers and craftsmen.

This synthesis has resulted in the creation of a sacred space which still has the power to affect us and help us tune into our divine potential.

This is an inspiring and informative book for anyone interested in religious architecture.

www.florisbooks.co.uk